The Wonder of What We Eat

COOKBOOK

FUN, HEALTHY RECIPES KIDS CAN COOK
AND LOVE — TO BUILD HEALTHY
HABITS, CONFIDENCE, AND JOYFUL
FAMILY MEALS

**Ritu Saluja-Sharma, MD
and Serena Sharma**

The Wonder of What We Eat Cookbook: Fun, Healthy Recipes Kids Can Cook and Love- To Build Healthy Habits, Confidence, and Joyful Family Meals
By Ritu Saluja-Sharma, MD, and Serena Sharma

Cover Illustration by Navdeep Kaur Komal

A companion cookbook to:

The Wonder of What We Eat: How Our Incredible Food, Our Incredible Bodies, And Our Incredible Planet Are Connected
By Ritu Saluja-Sharma, MD

and

The Wonder of What We Eat:Workbook: Activities and Reflections to Help Kids Build Healthy Habits and a Positive Relationship with Food
By Ritu Saluja-Sharma, MD, and Dylan Sharma

HEAD HEART HANDS

Published by Head Heart Hands LLC
Headhearthandsmd.com

Disclaimer
The content of this book is for general informational purposes only. Each person's physical, emotional, and spiritual condition is unique. The instruction in this book is not meant to be used, nor should it be used, to diagnose or treat any medical condition or to replace the services of your physician or other healthcare provider. The advice and strategies contained in the book may not be suitable for all readers. Neither the author, publisher, nor any of their employees or representatives guarantees the accuracy of information in this book or its usefulness to a particular reader, nor are they responsible for any damage or negative consequence that may result from any treatment, action taken, or inaction by any person reading or following the information in this book.

ISBN: 979-8-9990505-4-0

To the parents — in a world that doesn't make it easy to feed your kids healthy food, thank you for choosing to try. Every small choice, every homemade meal, every conversation about what's on the plate matters more than you know.

To every reader who learned, practiced, and is now ready to cook —your curiosity and care for your bodies (and the Earth!) make a difference every day. Each healthy bite helps you grow stronger now, feel better tomorrow, and build a healthier world for the future.

Here's to nourishing yourselves, your families, and our planet — one delicious meal at a time.

Food Is Energy

Food Is the Building Blocks of Our Body

Food Is Nutrients That Allow Our Cells to Function

Food Is Food for Our Microbiome

Food Is Information and Messages for Our Cells

Table of Contents

RECIPE LEVELS

⭐ Easy — Straightforward recipes with simple steps

⭐⭐ Medium — Some steps need extra care and more adult help

⭐⭐⭐ Advanced — Best for cooking together with an adult

*These stars are just a guide. Some "easy" recipes might still need adult help, especially when using knives or heat.

CHAPTER 1

BREAKFAST

Brilliant Banana Oatmeal

Makes: 4-5 servings

Difficulty:

This kid-approved banana oatmeal is fast and easy to make, has no added sugar or sweeteners, and tastes amazing! Perfect for before school or sports, this breakfast will fuel your brain and your body all morning long!

INGREDIENTS:

3 bananas

1 cup whole rolled oats (preferably organic)

1 ¾ cups water

½ teaspoon cinnamon

½ cup walnuts or other nuts (optional)

INSTRUCTIONS:

1. Mash 2 bananas with a fork in a large microwave-safe bowl. It's okay if a few small lumps remain. Add the oats and stir to mix them together.

2. Add the water and cinnamon. Stir again until everything looks mixed.

3. Microwave, uncovered, for 3–4 minutes. Watch carefully so it doesn't boil over — that's why you need a large bowl!

4. Stir in the walnuts (or other nuts or seeds, if you like). Top with slices of the third banana.

5. Sprinkle a little more cinnamon on top before serving.

BREAKFAST   **GLUTEN FREE, NO ADDED SUGAR, AND PLANT BASED**

Wholesome Whole Grain Pancakes

Makes: 2-3 servings

Difficulty:

These oatmeal pancakes are super easy to make because they come together in a blender! Not only that, but with more protein and nutrients than typical pancakes, these pancakes will keep you satisfied all morning, without any sugar highs and crashes.

INGREDIENTS:

2 cups whole rolled oats (preferably organic)

1 cup unsweetened organic soy milk (or other preferred milk)

½ cup greek yogurt (preferably organic and pasture raised)

1 egg

2 tablespoons real maple syrup, (not pancake syrup)

1 tablespoon avocado oil, (plus more for the pan)

1 teaspoon vanilla extract

2 teaspoons baking powder

1 teaspoon cinnamon

½ teaspoon sea salt

Fresh berries, for serving

Pecans, walnuts, homemade granola, or other nuts for serving (optional)

INSTRUCTIONS:

1. Combine the oats, soy milk, Greek yogurt, egg, maple syrup, avocado oil, vanilla, baking powder, cinnamon, and salt in a blender. Blend until the oats turn into flour and the batter looks smooth.

2. Pour about ⅓ cup of batter for each pancake onto a preheated, lightly greased griddle or pan. Watch for bubbles to form and the edges to look slightly cooked. Flip the pancakes and cook for 1–2 minutes on each side, or until golden brown.

3. Serve with fresh berries, nuts (or homemade granola — see page 12), and a drizzle of maple syrup.

Adapted from Oatmeal Pancakes recipe by Jeanine Donofrio (Love and Lemons).

BREAKFAST   **GLUTEN FREE**

The Very Best Granola

Makes: 14-20 servings

Difficulty:

This grain-free granola is delicious for breakfast or a snack. Sprinkle it on your oatmeal, yogurt, pancakes, or waffles, or just eat it by itself! Not only does it taste great, but it also contains lots of healthy fats, micronutrients, and protein.

INGREDIENTS:

2 cups unsweetened coconut flakes

2 cups sliced almonds

1 cup walnuts

1 cup whole raw pecans

½ cup raw pumpkin seeds (pepitas)

¼ cup chia seeds

1 teaspoon cinnamon

Big pinch salt

3 tablespoons pure maple syrup, not pancake syrup

1 tablespoon coconut oil

1 teaspoon vanilla

INSTRUCTIONS:

1. Mix coconut flakes, almonds, walnuts, pecans, pumpkin seeds, chia seeds, cinnamon, and a pinch of salt in a large bowl.

2. Combine maple syrup and coconut oil in a small microwave-safe bowl. Heat in the microwave for 15-25 seconds, or until the coconut oil has melted. Add vanilla and stir.

3. Combine the liquid mixture with the dry ingredients and stir.

4. Spread mixture onto a tray lined with parchment paper. Bake at 300°F for 10-12 minutes, or until the coconut flakes and almonds look slightly toasted.

5. Cool completely, then transfer to glass jars and store in the refrigerator. The granola will stay fresh for 2-3 weeks.

TIP:

Feel free to add or substitute your favorite nuts and seeds to customize this granola.

BREAKFAST

PLANT BASED AND GLUTEN FREE

Easiest Egg and Avocado Breakfast Sandwich

Makes: 1 serving

Difficulty:

This breakfast sandwich is super easy to make and is delicious! It contains whole grains, healthy protein, and healthy fats. Pair it with a plate of fruit to create an amazing breakfast!

INGREDIENTS:

1 egg (preferably organic and pasture raised).

1 tablespoon milk

Salt (to taste)

Pepper (to taste)

1 Ezeklal (or whole grain) English muffin

½ avocado

INSTRUCTIONS:

1. Crack an egg into a small microwave-safe bowl. Add milk, salt, and pepper. Use a fork or whisk to whisk vigorously until yolks, whites, and milk are combined.

2. Cover the bowl with a small plate and place it in the microwave. Cook on high for approximately 2 minutes and 15 seconds. (Depending on your microwave, you may need slightly more or less time.)

3. Toast an English muffin.

4. Cut avocado. (Cut the avocado lengthwise around the pit. Twist the halves to separate them. Use a spoon to remove the pit and to remove the avocado slices.)

5. Assemble the sandwich with the English muffin, egg patty, and avocado slices. Add additional salt and pepper as needed to taste.

WHY AVOCADOS?

Avocados are packed with healthy fats that help fuel your brain and keep you full of energy. They're also loaded with vitamins, fiber, and potassium, nutrients that keep your heart strong and digestive tract happy.

Their creamy texture makes them perfect for this breakfast sandwich.

TIP:

Feel free to use whole grain bread instead of the English muffin.

BREAKFAST

Perfect Chia Pudding

Makes: 1 serving

Difficulty:

Chia pudding is a healthy, fast, and delicious breakfast, and it's also fun to make! Customize with your favorite fruit, berries, and healthy toppings, and you have a complete meal!

INGREDIENTS:

2 tablespoons chia seeds

½ cup soy milk (unsweetened organic), or your preferred milk

2 teaspoons maple syrup

½ teaspoon vanilla extract

Berries for topping

Nuts for topping (optional)

Flavor Additions:

Chocolate: Add 1 tablespoon unsweetened cocoa powder

Chocolate coconut: Add 1 tablespoon unsweetened cocoa powder and 1 tablespoon unsweetened coconut flakes

Chocolate peanut butter: Add 1 tablespoon unsweetened cocoa powder and 1 tablespoon unsweetened peanut butter

Peanut butter and jelly: Add 1 tablespoon unsweetened peanut butter and 1 tablespoon fruit preserves

INSTRUCTIONS:

1. Combine chia seeds, soy milk, maple syrup, and vanilla in a jar or small glass. Use a fork or whisk to thoroughly mix.

2. Add desired flavor additions. Mix well.

3. Cover and place in the refrigerator overnight.

4. Top with berries and nuts (optional) when serving.

WHY CHIA SEEDS?

Why Chia Seeds? Chia seeds are tiny but packed with important nutrients your body needs. They're a great source of fiber, which helps keep your digestion healthy, and they provide plant-based protein to help you build muscle.

Chia seeds are also rich in omega-3 fatty acids, which are healthy fats that support your brain and heart. When mixed with liquid, they absorb it and form a gel, making them perfect for puddings, smoothies, or even to thicken recipes naturally.

BREAKFAST

PLANT BASED AND GLUTEN FREE

Breakfast Chocolate, Peanut Butter, and Banana Smoothie

Makes: 2 servings

Difficulty:

Looking for a quick and easy breakfast for when you are on the run? This smoothie tastes like a banana chocolate milkshake, but has no added sugar, and is a healthy breakfast option with fiber, protein, and lots of nutrients.

INGREDIENTS:

1 banana

½ cup uncooked whole rolled oats (preferably organic)

3 tablespoons peanut butter

1 cup organic unsweetened soy milk (or other milk of choice)

½ teaspoon cinnamon

1 tablespoon cocoa powder

3 handfuls of ice

INSTRUCTIONS:

1. Mix banana, oats, peanut butter, soy milk, cinnamon, and cocoa powder in a blender.

2. Blend until smooth.

3. Add ice (about 3 handfuls). Blend again until you reach your desired consistency.

4. Serve immediately and enjoy!

WHY BANANAS?

Bananas do a lot more than taste good! They are rich in potassium, which helps your muscles move and your heart beat properly. Their natural sugars give you quick energy, while fiber keeps your digestion healthy. Bananas also have vitamin B6, which supports brain function and mood. They're a simple fruit with serious power—fuel for both body and brain!

BREAKFAST   PLANT BASED, GLUTEN FREE, AND NO ADDED SUGAR

The Perfect Hard-Boiled Egg

Makes: 4 servings

Difficulty:

Want to learn a super-easy and guaranteed-to-work method to make hard-boiled eggs? This is for you!

INGREDIENTS:

4 Organic Pasture-Raised Eggs (preferably regenerative organic)

Water

Salt and Pepper to Taste

INSTRUCTIONS:

1. Place eggs in a pot, and cover eggs completely with water. Heat water and eggs until the water comes to a rolling boil.

2. Cover the pot. Turn off the heat.

3. Set a timer for 10-12 minutes. (Eggs cooked for 10 minutes will have creamier yolks. For eggs cooked for 12 minutes, the yolks will be drier. The photo is of an egg cooked for 12 minutes.)

4. Drain the hot water and rinse the eggs with cold water until cool enough to handle.

5. Peel and enjoy!

WHY ORGANIC PASTURE-RAISED EGGS?

Organic pasture-raised eggs come from hens that spend their days outdoors, in the sunshine, pecking around in the grass. Because they eat natural foods like plants and bugs, their eggs often have brighter yolks and more nutrients, like vitamin D and healthy omega-3 fats. "Organic" means the hens aren't given harmful chemicals, antibiotics, or genetically modified feed.

Some farms go even further by using regenerative organic practices, which help rebuild healthy soil, protect water, and care for the Earth while raising happy hens. Choosing these kinds of eggs is better for the chickens, the planet, and for you—it's a wholesome choice that supports healthy farms and happy animals.

BREAKFAST

Amazing Apple Oatmeal

Makes: 2-4 servings

Difficulty:

Made with just 5 ingredients, this apple oatmeal could not be any easier to make— and it's super healthy and delicious too. Naturally sweetened with smashed apples, this whole-grain breakfast will keep you satisfied and energized all morning.

INGREDIENTS:

2 apples

1 cup whole rolled oats (preferably organic)

1 ¾ cups water

Cinnamon

Walnuts, sliced almonds, seeds, or homemade granola for topping (optional)

INSTRUCTIONS:

1. Cut 2 apples into small bite-sized pieces, removing seeds and core. (Keep the peel on.) Place apples, oatmeal, and water into a large microwave-safe bowl.

2. Cook in microwave for 7-8 minutes, stirring halfway, until apples are soft. Watch the oatmeal while cooking, to make sure that it does not boil over. (This is why you need a large bowl.)

3. Mash about half of the apple pieces with a fork. Sprinkle cinnamon on top.

4. Optional: To make this a more balanced meal (with more protein and healthy fats), serve with nuts, seeds, or homemade granola on top.

WHY APPLES?

Apples aren't just delicious — they're little powerhouses of nutrition! They're packed with vitamin C to keep your immune system strong and your skin healthy, and they are a great source of fiber to help your digestion and keep you feeling full. The natural sugars in apples make them sweet to eat and also give you energy that lasts.

Plus, apples are full of antioxidants that protect your body's cells and support a healthy heart. With so many benefits in one fruit, it's no wonder people say, "An apple a day keeps the doctor away!"

BREAKFAST   GLUTEN FREE, NO ADDED SUGAR, AND PLANT BASED

Power Protein, Kale, and Berry Smoothie

Makes: 1-2 servings

Difficulty:

This smoothie has it all– lots of nutrients, lots of fiber, healthy fats, and lots of protein! Not only that, but it's so delicious, and will keep you full and energized all morning long!

INGREDIENTS:

1-2 handfuls baby kale

½ cup frozen blueberries

1 cup frozen raspberries

1 cup frozen strawberries

1 ½ cups soy milk, unsweetened and organic, (add more if needed, depending on desired consistency)

2 tablespoons chia seeds

2 tablespoons almond butter

INSTRUCTIONS:

1. Add kale, frozen berries, soy milk, chia seeds, and almond butter to a high-powered blender.

2. Blend until smooth and creamy.

3. Enjoy!

WHY BLUEBERRIES?

Blueberries may be small, but they're bursting with nutrition and flavor! Eating blueberries every day is one of the best things you can do for your health!

Blueberries are packed with vitamin C to support your immune system and fiber to help with healthy digestion. Their deep blue color comes from antioxidants called anthocyanins, which help protect your body's cells and keep your brain sharp.

Blueberries are naturally sweet, easy to toss into smoothies, yogurt, or oatmeal, and make every meal a little more colorful—and a lot more powerful!

BREAKFAST   PLANT BASED, NO ADDED SUGAR

On-the-Go Overnight Oats

Makes: 1 serving

Difficulty:

Overnight oats are super easy to make, and they are a nutritious and delicious breakfast. Not only that, they can be customized in countless ways! This version uses frozen cherries, which thaw by morning, and give the oats natural sweetness!

INGREDIENTS:

½ cup rolled oats (preferably organic)

½ cup soy milk (preferably unsweetened and organic), or other milk of your choice

1 tablespoon chia seeds

¼ cup frozen fruit (we love using frozen sweet cherries!)

1 teaspoon real maple syrup (optional)

INSTRUCTIONS:

1. Add oats, soy milk, chia seeds, and frozen fruit to a small cup or jar. If desired, add the maple syrup for extra sweetness. Use a fork or whisk to mix thoroughly.

2. Cover. Refrigerate overnight.

3. Add your desired toppings before serving.

TOPPING IDEAS:

Almond Joy: unsweetened coconut flakes, sliced almonds, a few chocolate chips

Apple Pie: apple slices, cinnamon, pecans

Peanut Butter and Jelly: peanut butter and jam (preferably without added sweeteners

Chocolate Hazelnut and Banana: Banana slices and a scoop of homemade chocolate hazelnut spread (recipe page 120).

Blueberry Goodness: Blueberries and walnuts

WHY OATS?

Oats are a breakfast classic for good reason! They are naturally whole grain, high in fiber, and packed with important minerals like magnesium and iron. That fiber (especially beta-glucan) supports healthy digestion, helps you feel full, and can even lower cholesterol for heart health. Oats also provide steady energy thanks to their complex carbs, plus B vitamins and plant-based protein to fuel your day.

Not all oats are the same, though. Rolled and steel-cut oats are less processed than instant, which means they keep more of their natural texture, nutrients, and slow-digesting carbs. This helps avoid blood sugar spikes and keeps energy levels steady. For the best nutrition, rolled or steel-cut oats are the way to go.

BREAKFAST   **GLUTEN FREE, NO ADDED SUGAR, AND PLANT BASED**

Fabulous Fruit and Nut Muesli

Makes: 22-33 servings

Difficulty:

Want an easy alternative to boxed cereal for breakfast? This muesli is a much better option! Made with all whole foods, this balanced meal will keep you energized and satisfied all morning long!

INGREDIENTS:

4 cups whole rolled oats (preferably organic)

1 cup chopped pecans

1 cup pumpkin seeds (pepitas)

2 cups sliced almonds

1 cup unsweetened coconut flakes

1 cup hemp seeds

1 cup dried cranberries, or raisins, (unsweetened and without added oils)

2 teaspoons (heaping) ground cinnamon

½ teaspoon salt

3 tablespoons pure maple syrup

1 tablespoon coconut oil

2 teaspoons pure vanilla extract

Your favorite berries for serving

Milk for serving (organic unsweetened soy milk pictured here)

INSTRUCTIONS:

1. Combine oats, pecans, pumpkin seeds, almonds, coconut flakes, hemp seeds, cranberries, cinnamon, and salt in a large bowl. Mix.

2. Combine pure maple syrup (not table or pancake syrup) and coconut oil in a small microwave-safe bowl.

3. Microwave for 15 seconds (or more, depending on your microwave) until the coconut oil has melted.

4. Add vanilla to the coconut oil mixture.

5. Pour the coconut oil mixture over the oat and nut mixture. Stir until everything is evenly coated.

6. Spread the mixture on a parchment-lined baking sheet. Bake at 300°F for 10–15 minutes, or until the nuts and coconut look lightly toasted.

7. Serve with your favorite berries and milk. Store the leftover muesli in glass jars in the fridge for a quick and easy breakfast.

TIP

Feel free to add or substitute your favorite nuts, seeds, and fruit to customize this muesli.

BREAKFAST

PLANT BASED AND GLUTEN FREE

Superfood Chocolate Oatmeal

Makes: 4 servings

Difficulty:

Chocolate for breakfast? Why, yes, what a wonderful idea! And not only is this chocolate oatmeal tasty, but it's easy to make and super healthy too!

INGREDIENTS:

1 cup whole rolled oats (preferably organic)

1 ¾ cups water

1 teaspoon cinnamon

2 tablespoons cocoa powder

1 whole pitted date

½ cup walnuts

4 tablespoons pumpkin seeds

2 cups berries (blueberries, strawberries, or raspberries would all work well)

2 tablespoons pure maple syrup (optional for additional sweetness)

INSTRUCTIONS:

1. Mix oats, water, cinnamon, and cocoa powder in a microwave-safe bowl until well combined.

2. Chop the pitted date into tiny pieces and mix them into the oats mixture.

3. Cook the oats mixture in the microwave on high for 3-4 minutes, until it is bubbly and thicker.

4. Add walnuts and pumpkin seeds to the cooked oats.

5. Spoon the oatmeal into bowls and top each with ½ cup of berries.

6. Taste before adding any maple syrup—depending on your berries, it may already be sweet enough. If desired, add about ½ tablespoon of maple syrup to each bowl and mix.

7. Make ahead: Store the oatmeal (before adding berries) in the refrigerator for up to 2–3 days.

TIP

Feel free to add or substitute your favorite nuts, seeds, and fruit to customize this oatmeal.

BREAKFAST   PLANT BASED AND GLUTEN FREE

Irresistible Chocolate Muesli

Makes: 20-30 servings

Difficulty:

This chocolate muesli feels like a treat in the morning, but it's actually healthy too! Made with whole grains, nuts, and seeds, this muesli is packed with protein and healthy fats. Serve with milk and berries for a filling and healthy breakfast!

INGREDIENTS:

4 cups whole rolled oats (preferably organic)

2 cups sliced almonds

1 cup pecans

1 cup hemp seeds

2 cups large, unsweetened coconut flakes

1 teaspoon fine salt

2 teaspoons cinnamon

3 tablespoons maple syrup

1 tablespoon melted coconut oil

2 teaspoons vanilla extract

½ cup dark chocolate chips

INSTRUCTIONS:

1. Combine oats, almonds, pecans, hemp seeds, coconut flakes, salt, and cinnamon in a large bowl. Mix.

2. Combine pure maple syrup (not table syrup) and coconut oil in a small microwave-safe bowl.

3. Microwave for 15 seconds (or more, depending on your microwave) until the coconut oil has melted.

4. Add vanilla to the coconut oil mixture.

5. Add the coconut oil mixture to the oats and nuts mixture. Stir until evenly coated.

6. Spread mixture on a baking sheet lined with parchment paper, and bake at 300°F for 10-15 minutes, or until the nuts and coconut look slightly toasted.

7. Remove from oven and cool. Stir in chocolate chips once the muesli has cooled completely.

8. Serve with your favorite berries and milk.

9. Store the leftover muesli in glass jars in the fridge for a quick and easy breakfast. One batch will make over 20 servings.

BREAKFAST

PLANT BASED AND GLUTEN FREE

Protein Packed Waffles

Makes: 5 servings

Difficulty:  ★ ★

Most waffles are made of just refined carbohydrates and sugar, which can cause energy spikes and crashes! These waffles are different! Packed with protein and healthy fats, these delicious waffles will give you lasting energy and keep you satisfied all morning!

INGREDIENTS:

2 cups almond flour

2 teaspoons baking powder

1 teaspoon cinnamon

½ teaspoon salt

2 tablespoons arrowroot starch

2 eggs

2 tablespoons extra virgin olive oil

4 tablespoons real maple syrup (not table or pancake syrup)

1 cup soy milk (unsweetened and organic), or other preferred milk

1 teaspoon pure vanilla extract

2-3 cups fresh berries (blueberries, strawberries, or raspberries)

Additional real maple syrup (optional as needed for sweetness)

Butter (optional for serving)

INSTRUCTIONS:

1. Combine all dry ingredients in a large bowl: almond flour, baking powder, cinnamon, salt, and arrowroot starch. Mix.

2. Add wet ingredients: eggs, olive oil, maple syrup, soy milk, and vanilla extract. Mix until the batter is smooth.

3. Preheat the waffle iron.

4. Pour about ¼ cup of batter into the center of the heated waffle iron. (This amount won't spread to the edges—it makes slightly smaller waffles that can fit in your toaster.)

5. Cook according to your waffle iron's instructions, or until golden brown. Remove carefully.

6. Serve with berries. You can also add maple syrup and butter, if desired.

TIP

Top these waffles with "The Very Best Granola" (recipe is on page 12) to make them even more delicious.

BREAKFAST

GLUTEN FREE

CHAPTER 2

LUNCH

Rainbow Chickpea Salad

Makes: 4-6 servings

Difficulty:

Want to eat more colors (more nutrients)? Then add this easy and delicious chickpea salad to your rotation! This easy rainbow chickpea salad is packed with nutrition, and it's so easy to make as a quick lunch or side dish.

INGREDIENTS:

2 cans (15 oz each) chickpeas, rinsed and drained

½ cucumber, chopped

½ red onion, chopped

1 yellow, orange, or red bell pepper, chopped

½ cup kalamata olives, pitted and chopped

¼ cup fresh parsley, chopped

⅓ cup extra virgin olive oil

Juice of 2 lemons

½ teaspoon salt

½ teaspoon black pepper

¼ cup feta cheese (optional)

INSTRUCTIONS:

1. Mix chickpeas, cucumber, onion, bell pepper, olives, and parsley in a large bowl.

2. Whisk together the olive oil, lemon juice, salt, and pepper in a small bowl or measuring cup.

3. Pour the dressing over the chickpea mixture and gently toss to coat.

4. Add feta cheese before serving, if desired.

WHY CHICKPEAS?

Chickpeas are small, delicious, round beans that are packed with nutrition. They are a great source of protein to help build strong muscles. They are filled with fiber, which keeps your digestion healthy and helps you feel full longer.

Chickpeas also provide important vitamins and minerals like iron, magnesium, and folate—nutrients your body needs to stay active and strong. Chickpeas are also super versatile—you can eat them plain or in salads and soups, blend them into hummus, or even roast them for a crunchy snack!

LUNCH

PLANT BASED

Amazingly Easy Avocado Toast

Makes: 2-3 servings

Difficulty:

Made with just 4-5 ingredients, this avocado toast is a fast and delicious option for lunch or breakfast! Serve with some fruit or veggies and a quick bean salad, and you have a complete meal!

INGREDIENTS:

2 avocados

4 tablespoons lemon juice (about the juice from 1 lemon)

Salt to taste

Whole grain bread (whole grain sourdough works well here)

Crushed red pepper (optional if you want to make it spicy)

INSTRUCTIONS:

1. Cut the avocados. (Cut each avocado lengthwise around the pit. Twist the halves to separate them. Use a spoon to remove the pit and to remove the avocado slices.) Smash the avocados using a fork.

2. Add lemon juice and salt to taste. Mix with the avocado.

3. Toast 4 pieces of whole-grain bread.

4. Spread the avocado mixture on the toast.

5. Sprinkle with crushed red pepper for spice. (Optional).

WHY WHOLE GRAIN SOURDOUGH BREAD?

Whole grain sourdough bread isn't just tasty—it's full of goodness for your body! Because it's made from whole grains, it means more fiber, protein, and nutrients to keep your energy steady and your digestion healthy.

The "sourdough" part comes from a natural fermentation process that uses friendly bacteria and yeast to help the dough rise. This makes the bread easier to digest and can even help your body absorb more nutrients from the grains. Plus, it has a delicious, slightly tangy flavor that makes every sandwich or toast extra special!

LUNCH

PLANT BASED

Easy and Healthy, Creamy Tomato Soup

Makes: 4 servings

Difficulty:

This tomato soup is dairy-free, but creamy and delicious. Kid-approved and fast and easy to make, this tomato soup is a healthier spin on a family favorite comfort food.

INGREDIENTS:

2 tablespoons extra virgin olive oil

1 medium red onion, chopped

4 cloves garlic, chopped

¼ cup fresh basil leaves (optional)

1 large can (28 oz) peeled tomatoes

2 cups vegetable broth

½ teaspoon salt, or more to taste

½ teaspoon sugar (optional)

½ cup raw, unsalted cashews

INSTRUCTIONS:

1. Sauté (cook in a little oil) the onion and garlic in olive oil over medium heat until the onion is soft and translucent.

2. Add basil leaves, peeled tomatoes, and vegetable broth. Bring to a boil, then reduce the heat and simmer, covered, for 20 minutes.

3. Stir in the salt and sugar.

4. Add the cashews to a blender. Carefully pour the tomato mixture into the blender and cover. Use a towel on top to protect yourself from any splatters. Carefully blend. Start slowly and then gradually increase speed until the mixture is smooth and creamy.

5. Pour the soup into bowls and serve.

Adapted from Easy Vegan Tomato Soup recipe by Nora (Noracooks).

LUNCH

PLANT BASED

The Tastiest Mayo-Free Tuna Salad

Makes: 4-6 servings

Difficulty:

This tuna salad is light and fresh, and tastes so delicious, you won't miss the white stuff! Easy to make, and healthy too— this tuna salad makes a perfect family-friendly lunch!

INGREDIENTS:

2 cans (10oz) Skipjack wild tuna (pole and line caught)

1 cup chopped celery

¼ cup chopped cilantro

4 chopped green onions

3 tablespoons extra virgin olive oil

2 tablespoons lemon juice (juice from ½ lemon)

½ teaspoon ground cumin

Black pepper to taste

Salt to taste

Crushed red pepper to taste (optional)

INSTRUCTIONS:

1. Mix tuna, celery, cilantro, and green onions. Stir in extra virgin olive oil and lemon juice.

2. Add cumin and black pepper. Add salt to taste. (Be careful not to put too much salt if the canned tuna was in salted water.) Mix gently.

3. Serve on toasted whole grain bread (whole grain sourdough works well here). Top with crushed red pepper (optional).

WHY POLE AND LINE CAUGHT SKIPJACK TUNA?

Tuna is a great source of lean protein and omega-3 fatty acids, which help keep your brain, heart, and muscles healthy. It also provides important nutrients like vitamin D, iron, and selenium.

But not all tuna is the same! Some kinds can have higher levels of mercury, a metal that's not good for our bodies if we eat too much of it. Skipjack tuna is a smaller species that naturally has less mercury, making it a safer and smarter choice, especially for kids.

Whenever you can, it's also best to choose skipjack tuna that is pole-and-line caught. In this traditional method of fishing, the fish are caught one at a time, which helps protect other sea creatures and keeps the ocean's ecosystems healthy.

LUNCH

Classic Caprese Sandwich

Makes: 4 sandwiches

Difficulty:

This easy-to-assemble sandwich is made with simple ingredients, yet it's so flavorful. It's a fast and delicious lunch option that can even be packed in a lunchbox. Pair this sandwich with some veggies and a bean salad, and you have a full meal.

INGREDIENTS:

8 oz ball of fresh mozzarella cheese, sliced

1-2 fresh tomatoes, sliced (vine ripened, Roma, or Heirloom work well)

Fresh basil leaves

Whole grain bread (whole grain sourdough or a whole grain baguette work well here)

Salt and fresh ground pepper to taste

Extra virgin olive oil

INSTRUCTIONS:

Panini style:
1. Assemble sandwiches with sliced mozzarella, sliced tomatoes, and fresh basil on whole-grain sourdough bread.

2. Add salt and pepper to taste.

3. Drizzle the outside of the sandwiches with 1 tablespoon of extra virgin olive oil. Use a panini press or a pan to toast the sandwiches.

Baguette or Sandwich style:
1. Lightly toast the baguette or bread slices.

2. Assemble sandwiches with sliced tomatoes, mozzarella, and fresh basil.

3. Add salt and pepper to taste.

LUNCH

VEGETARIAN

Protein-Packed Pasta and Peas

Makes: 4 servings

Difficulty:

This quick and easy, one-pot pasta meal is made with simple ingredients, but it's packed with protein, fiber, and nutrients. Best part—it's delicious and kid-approved!

INGREDIENTS:

1 tablespoon extra virgin olive oil

1 small red onion, chopped

2 cloves garlic, finely chopped

1 bag (16oz) frozen peas

2 cups vegetable broth (or more if needed)

1 box (8oz) of chickpea or lentil pasta

1 teaspoon salt (more or less to taste)

Black pepper to taste

Crushed red pepper to taste (optional)

½ cup grated parmesan cheese (optional)

INSTRUCTIONS:

1. Sauté onion and garlic in olive oil until the onion is slightly translucent.

2. Add frozen peas and 2 cups of broth. Bring to a gentle boil. Stir in pasta and salt.

3. Reduce the heat to a simmer, cover, and cook until the pasta is tender and most of the liquid has been absorbed, stirring frequently. If the liquid evaporates too quickly or the pasta isn't fully cooked, add more broth, about ½ cup at a time, until the pasta is done and the texture is creamy.

4. Season with black pepper and crushed red pepper to taste. Stir in Parmesan cheese, if desired.

WHY PEAS?

Peas may be small, but they're packed with big nutrition! They are a great source of plant-based protein, about 8 grams of protein per cup, which helps your body build and repair muscles. They're also full of fiber, which keeps your digestion healthy and helps you feel full.

Peas also provide important nutrients like vitamin C, vitamin K, and iron, all of which support strong bones, a healthy immune system, and steady energy.

LUNCH   PLANT BASED

Perfectly Easy Pasta Pomodoro

Makes: 4 servings

Difficulty:

Made with simple ingredients, this pasta with fresh tomatoes and basil is a snap to make— and it's absolutely delicious.

INGREDIENTS:

1 box (8 oz) lentil, chickpea, or whole grain pasta

2 tablespoons extra virgin olive oil

½ red onion, chopped

4 cloves garlic, finely chopped

1 pound vine-ripened tomatoes (about 3–4 medium), chopped into small pieces

8-10 fresh basil leaves, chopped (optional)

Salt and pepper to taste

Crushed red pepper (optional) to taste

Parmesan cheese (optional)

INSTRUCTIONS:

1. Cook pasta according to the instructions.

2. Sauté onion and garlic in olive oil until the onion is slightly translucent.

3. Add chopped tomatoes and basil leaves. Cook at medium-low heat, stirring frequently until the tomatoes are tender and saucy. Add salt and pepper to taste. Add crushed red pepper and parmesan, if desired.

4. Add tomato mixture to pasta and serve.

WHY LENTIL PASTA?

Lentil pasta looks and tastes a lot like regular pasta, but it's made from lentils instead of wheat, so it's extra nutritious!

One cup of cooked lentil pasta can have around 15 grams of protein (compared to about 7 grams in typical pasta), which helps your body build strong muscles. One cup of lentil pasta also contains about 6 grams of fiber (compared to about 3 grams in typical pasta), which keeps your digestion healthy and helps you feel full longer.

Lentil pasta is also a good source of iron, potassium, and B vitamins, all important for steady energy. Because it's made from lentils, it's naturally gluten-free and gives your meal a hearty, satisfying boost.

LUNCH

PLANT BASED

Pesto Pasta Twirls

Makes: 4-6 servings

Difficulty:

This homemade pesto is so flavorful and so fast to make, ready in less than 5 minutes. An easy lunch or side dish, this pasta dish is loaded with nutrients, fiber, protein, and healthy fats.

INGREDIENTS:

1 box lentil, chickpea, or whole grain pasta (fusilli works well here)

1 ½ cups baby spinach leaves

¾ cup fresh basil leaves

½ cup walnuts

4 cloves garlic (peeled)

¾ teaspoon salt

½ teaspoon freshly ground black pepper

1 tablespoon fresh lemon juice

½ cup extra virgin olive oil

INSTRUCTIONS:

1. Make pasta according to package directions.

2. Add spinach, basil, walnuts, garlic, salt, black pepper, lemon juice, and olive oil to a food processor. Blend all of the ingredients until smooth.

3. Mix the desired amount of pesto sauce with the pasta, and add additional salt, if desired. Pesto pasta can be served warm or cold.

4. Store the leftover pesto sauce in the fridge for up to 2 days.

WHY BASIL?

Basil isn't just a pretty green herb—it's full of flavor and nutrition! It adds a fresh, slightly sweet taste to foods like pasta, pizza, and salads, plus it's rich in vitamins A, K, and C, which help support healthy skin, strong bones, and a strong immune system. It also contains antioxidants, natural plant compounds that help protect your body's cells. Fresh basil can turn an ordinary dish into something extraordinary and super healthy!

LUNCH

PLANT BASED

Very Easy Vegetable and Rotisserie Chicken Salad

Makes: 6 servings

Difficulty:

This salad is colorful, easy, kid-approved, and a complete meal. Made with your favorite greens, a variety of veggies, beans, seeds, healthy fats, and pieces of chicken-- this salad has it all! This salad is proof that eating salad does NOT mean just eating lettuce!

INGREDIENTS:

Baby Kale or Spinach leaves

Cucumbers, sliced

Carrots, sliced

Bell peppers (red, orange, or yellow), sliced

Sugar snap Peas

Avocado, sliced

Olives

Canned chickpeas, rinsed and drained

Rotisserie chicken breast (shredded)

Pumpkin seeds (without added oils), sprinkled on top for crunch

Spicy Cashew Dressing (optional):
1 cup fresh cilantro
2 cloves garlic, peeled
1 inch piece of fresh ginger root, peeled
2 tablespoons maple syrup
⅓ cup cashew butter
1 tablespoon extra virgin olive oil
2 tablespoons lime juice
½ teaspoon salt (or more to taste)
A pinch of chili flakes

INSTRUCTIONS:

1. Assemble salad with greens, veggies, and your favorite toppings.

2. To make the dressing: combine all ingredients in a food processor and mix. Add water if needed to thin out the mixture.

TIP:

This salad is easy to put together and can be customized to your liking!

Want to add beets? No problem! Want to swap some different seeds for the crunch? Go for it!

Just remember to start with some nutrient-dense greens (we prefer baby spinach or kale), add a variety of chopped veggies, add some healthy fats (we added avocado, olives, and pumpkin seeds), add some beans and seeds (for protein and fiber), and then, if you choose, add some shredded rotisserie chicken breast on top.

Top with your favorite dressing (any vinaigrette made with olive oil would work well here, or you can try this spicy cashew dressing), and you have a complete meal! This salad is so much more delicious than most restaurant salads, and is much healthier too!

LUNCH

The Easiest Bean Salad

Makes: 6-8 servings

Difficulty:

This bean salad is so fast to make, and it's a kid-favorite and crowd-favorite. Loaded with fiber and protein, this salad can be a healthy lunch or side dish that goes with almost any meal.

INGREDIENTS:

2 cans (15 oz each) chickpeas, rinsed and drained

1 can (15 oz) black beans, rinsed and drained

4 green onions, chopped

½ cup fresh cilantro, chopped

Juice of 2 lemons (about 8 tablespoons)

1 teaspoon cumin

½ teaspoon salt, or to taste

½ teaspoon black pepper

INSTRUCTIONS:

1. Combine chickpeas, black beans, green onions, and cilantro in a large bowl.

2. Add the lemon juice, cumin, salt, and pepper.

3. Mix well to combine and serve.

WHY BLACK BEANS?

Black beans are delicious, nutritious, and so versatile! They're packed with plant-based protein—about 15 grams per cup—to help your body build and repair muscles. They're also rich in fiber, with around 15 grams per cup, which supports healthy digestion and keeps you feeling full and energized.

Black beans provide important nutrients like iron, magnesium, and folate, all of which help your body make energy and keep your heart healthy. Their deep color comes from natural plant compounds called antioxidants, which help protect your cells. Whether in tacos, soups, or salads, black beans add flavor, color, and lasting nutrition to any meal!

LUNCH

PLANT BASED

The Best Bruschetta

Makes: 3-4 servings

Difficulty:

Bruschetta is a classic Italian appetizer, but it can be a delicious and healthy lunch option too! Serve with a side of veggies and an easy bean salad, and you have a balanced meal!

INGREDIENTS:

1 pint grape or cherry tomatoes, chopped

¼ cup fresh basil, chopped

3 garlic cloves, finely chopped

2 tablespoons extra virgin olive oil

Salt to taste

Whole grain bread (whole grain sourdough works well here)

INSTRUCTIONS:

1. Chop tomatoes, basil, and garlic and mix. Add olive oil and salt to taste.

2. Toast slices of whole-grain bread.

3. Top toast with the tomato mixture and serve.

TIP:

Store the leftovers separately from the bread, for up to 2 days, but best when fresh.

WHY TOMATOES?

Tomatoes are bright, juicy, and bursting with nutrients your body loves. They're an excellent source of vitamin C, which helps keep your immune system strong, and vitamin A, which supports good vision and healthy skin. Tomatoes also contain lycopene, a natural red pigment that acts as a powerful antioxidant—helping to protect your cells and keep you healthy.

Protein and Nutrient Packed Quinoa Salad

Makes: 6-8 servings

Difficulty:

This delicious quinoa salad is loaded with whole grains, protein, and healthy fats. Make a big batch and pack it for lunch this week, or eat it as a side– either way, you will want to add this recipe to your rotation.

INGREDIENTS:

1 cup quinoa (any color)

2 cups water

4 cups shredded cabbage (any color)

2 cups shredded carrots

1 red, orange, or yellow bell pepper, chopped

½ cup fresh cilantro, chopped

1 cup cooked and shelled edamame or green peas (or both)

4 green onions, chopped

½ cup dry roasted and salted peanuts

Dressing:

¼ cup extra virgin olive oil

¼ cup honey

2 tablespoons soy sauce

1 tablespoon natural peanut butter (no added sugar or palm oil)

1 tablespoon ginger (grated or minced)

2 cloves garlic (grated or minced)

½ teaspoon salt

Pinch of red pepper flakes (optional)

INSTRUCTIONS:

1. Rinse and drain quinoa. In a large pot, combine rinsed quinoa with water and bring to a boil. When water is boiling, cover, turn down the heat to low, and simmer until quinoa is cooked and has absorbed all of the water (about 10 minutes). Let quinoa cool.

2. Combine shredded cabbage and carrots. (To reduce chopping, you can also buy a pre-shredded cabbage and carrot mixture.) Add bell pepper, cilantro, edamame (or peas), and green onions. Mix in half of the peanuts.

3. Whisk the dressing in a small measuring cup or bowl by combining the olive oil, honey, soy sauce, peanut butter, ginger, garlic, salt, and red pepper flakes (optional)..

4. Assemble salad by mixing the quinoa and vegetables. Add dressing and mix well. Add additional salt and red pepper flakes to taste. Garnish with the leftover peanuts.

WHY QUINOA?

Quinoa (pronounced keen-wah) is a super seed (which also counts as a whole grain), which is packed with protein and fiber. Plus, it's rich in iron and magnesium, which help keep your energy up and your body healthy. It cooks quickly (similar to rice), and tastes great in salads, bowls, or as a side dish!

LUNCH

PLANT BASED

CHAPTER 3

DINNER

The Best Black Bean Quesadillas

Makes: 4 servings   **Difficulty:** ★ ★ ★

This meal has it all! These black bean and vegetable quesadillas are loaded with fiber, protein, and nutrients, and are so delicious! Kid-approved and easy to make, these quesadillas make an easy and nutritious dinner (and the leftovers can even be packed for lunch!)

INGREDIENTS:

Extra virgin olive oil

1 (10 oz) box baby spinach

2 (15 oz each) cans black beans, rinsed and drained

2 bell peppers (red, orange, or yellow), sliced

1 package (8oz) mushrooms, sliced

2 teaspoons cumin (1 teaspoon for the spinach and bean mixture, and 1 teaspoon for the peppers and mushrooms mixture)

1 teaspoon salt, or more to taste

Sprinkle cayenne pepper (optional)

8 corn tortillas

1 package (8 oz) shredded cheddar cheese

Pickled Jalapeños for serving (optional)

Guacamole for serving (optional)

Pico for serving (optional)

INSTRUCTIONS:

1. Heat 1 tablespoon extra virgin olive oil in a pan. Add spinach, cover, and turn down the heat to low. Over the next couple of minutes, allow the spinach to wilt and shrink, tossing the spinach intermittently, so that all of the leaves get rotated.

2. Add rinsed and drained black beans. Add 1 teaspoon cumin, ½ teaspoon salt, and cayenne pepper (if desired). Stir until heated. Transfer the mixture to a bowl.

3. In the same pan, heat 1 tablespoon of olive oil on medium-high. Add mushrooms and peppers, 1 teaspoon of cumin, and ½ teaspoon salt. Sauté until the peppers and mushrooms are cooked.

4. Add a teaspoon of extra virgin olive oil to a skillet. To assemble each quesadilla, place the tortilla in the skillet. On one half of the tortilla, add bean and spinach mixture, a sprinkle of cheddar cheese, and mushroom/bell pepper mixture. Fold the other half of the tortilla on top. Allow cheese to melt, and tortilla to slightly toast, using the spatula to press the quesadilla together. Flip the quesadilla to toast the other side. Quesadillas are ready when tortillas are lightly toasted and cheese has melted.

5. Serve with homemade guacamole (recipe page 124), homemade pico (recipe page 118), and jalapeno peppers (if desired).

DINNER   VEGETARIAN

Mighty Minestrone Soup

Makes: 6-8 servings

Difficulty:

Minestrone soup is the perfect one-pot meal-- it's delicious, healthy, kid-approved, and easy. Plus, the leftovers can be packed for lunch for the whole week! This minestrone soup recipe contains lots of veggies, beans, greens, herbs, and lentil pasta- providing lots of nutrition and lots of flavor.

INGREDIENTS:

2 tablespoons avocado oil

1 large red onion, chopped

4-5 stalks celery, chopped

4-5 carrots, chopped

4 cloves garlic, finely chopped

3 cans (15 oz each) kidney beans, or a mix of kidney beans and white beans, rinsed and drained

1 box (8oz) lentil or chickpea pasta (bowties, fusilli, or shells work well)

1 large can (28 oz) crushed tomatoes

1 tablespoon dried oregano (or fresh if available)

1 tablespoon dried basil (or fresh if available)

1 teaspoon salt, or more to taste

½ teaspoon fresh ground black pepper, or more to taste

6 cups vegetable broth

1 box (10oz) baby kale leaves (or baby spinach works too)

INSTRUCTIONS:

1. Sauté the onion, celery, carrots, and garlic in avocado oil in a large pot (a cast-iron pot works well).

2. Cook until the onions are soft and translucent. Add the beans, pasta, and crushed tomatoes. Add the oregano, basil, salt, and pepper. Pour in the vegetable broth and stir to combine.

3. Bring the soup to a boil. Once boiling, cover, reduce the heat to low, and simmer for about 20 minutes.

4. Add the kale and stir until it has completely wilted. Season with more salt and pepper to taste. Enjoy!

FUN FACT:

In a place called Sardinia, Italy, which is recognized as one of the places in the world where people live the longest, often reaching over 100 years, families often make minestrone soup filled with beans and veggies. It is believed that eating meals like this is part of what helps to keep them healthy for so long.

DINNER

PLANT BASED

Better-Than-the-Drive-Thru Grilled Chicken Sandwiches

Makes: 4-6 servings

Difficulty:

Craving a fast-food chicken sandwich? Check out this recipe to make a healthier, delicious version at home! Kid-approved and easy, this grilled chicken sandwich recipe is a winner!

INGREDIENTS:

2 cups pickle juice, (or enough to cover)

1 teaspoon garlic powder

1 teaspoon smoked paprika

2 boneless, skinless chicken breasts (preferably organic)

Avocado oil for grill

4 whole grain buns

OPTIONAL TOPPINGS:

Pickle slices

Lettuce

Tomatoes (sliced)

Onions (sliced)

INSTRUCTIONS:

1. Mix pickle juice, garlic powder, and paprika to make the marinade.

2. Slice each chicken breast in half horizontally to create 4 thin cutlets, each about ½ inch thick. This will help the chicken cook evenly on the grill. Depending on the size of the breasts and your desired cutlet size, cut them in half if needed. Add chicken pieces to the marinade.

3. Marinate the chicken breasts in the fridge for 4-8 hours.

4. When ready to grill, prep the grill with avocado oil. Preheat grill to 400°F. Grill for about 6 minutes on each side. Use a meat thermometer to check that the internal temperature is over 165°F to ensure that the chicken is properly cooked.

5. To assemble the sandwiches, start with a whole-grain bun, add grilled chicken, pickle slices, and desired toppings. Lettuce, tomato, and onion work well.

6. Round out the meal with air-fried French fries (recipe page 96) and a simple veggie side for a wholesome twist on fast food.

DINNER

Sizzlin' Shrimp Tacos

Makes: 4-6 servings

Difficulty:

These shrimp tacos are filled with fresh ingredients and flavor, and they are also super fast to make! Serve them with fresh guacamole to make this meal even more delicious and healthy!

INGREDIENTS:

For the Slaw:

3 cups shredded cabbage (any color)

1 mango, chopped into small pieces

¼ cup cilantro, chopped

½ teaspoon salt

2 limes, juiced

For the Shrimp:

1 pound shrimp, deveined with tail removed

1 teaspoon ground cumin

¼ teaspoon oregano

1 teaspoon smoked paprika

1 teaspoon fine salt

½ teaspoon ground black pepper

Pinch of cayenne pepper or crushed red pepper (optional)

1 lime, juiced

1 tablespoon avocado oil

8 corn tortillas

INSTRUCTIONS:

1. Prep the slaw by mixing the cabbage, mango, cilantro, salt, and lime juice.

2. Assemble shrimp seasoning by mixing cumin, oregano, paprika, salt, pepper, cayenne pepper, and lime juice. Toss shrimp in seasoning.

3. Heat the skillet on medium-high, and add 1 tablespoon avocado oil. Add shrimp in a single layer. Sauté for 1-2 minutes on each side, or until completely cooked.

4. Warm the corn tortillas (either in a pan on the stove or very lightly in the toaster oven).

5. Assemble the tacos with the shrimp and slaw mixture. Serve with homemade guacamole (recipe page 124).

DINNER

Garden Fresh Veggie Chili With Avocado

Makes: 6-8 servings

Difficulty:

A pot of this veggie-packed chili is a delicious and complete meal! Packed with lots of veggies, plant-based protein, and avocado for some healthy fat– this satisfying meal is a great dinner! And the leftovers can be used for lunch for the next few days, too!

INGREDIENTS:

- 2 tablespoons avocado oil
- 1 medium red onion, chopped
- 1 large red bell pepper, chopped
- 4 medium carrots, chopped
- 4 cloves garlic, finely chopped
- 1 teaspoon salt (or more for taste)
- 2 tablespoons chili powder
- 2 teaspoons ground cumin

- 1 ½ teaspoons smoked paprika
- 1 teaspoon dried oregano
- 3 cans (15 oz each) kidney beans, rinsed and drained
- 1 large can (28oz) crushed fire-roasted tomatoes
- 2 cups vegetable broth
- 1 box (5oz) baby spinach leaves
- ¼ cup cilantro, chopped
- Avocado, chopped (optional for serving)

INSTRUCTIONS:

1. Heat the avocado oil in a large pot over medium-high heat. Add the onion, bell peppers, and carrots. Sauté until the onions are soft and translucent..

2. Add garlic, salt, chili powder, cumin, paprika, and oregano, and sauté for another minute.

3. Add beans and crushed tomatoes. Stir. Add vegetable broth. Stir.

4. Bring soup to a boil. When boiling, cover, reduce the heat to low, and simmer for 20 minutes.

5. Add spinach leaves and stir until they are completely wilted. Add cilantro.

6. Top each bowl with chopped avocado when serving.

DINNER   **PLANT BASED**

Family Favorite Turkey Burgers

Makes: 6 servings

Difficulty:

Think turkey burgers are boring and dry? Or that you need loads of fatty meat to make a good burger? Think again! These easy turkey burgers are super juicy—thanks to the grated onion—and bursting with flavor from garlic and cilantro. Made with lean turkey breast, they're a lighter, better-for-you burger option the whole family will love.

INGREDIENTS:

1 pound ground turkey breast (preferably organic)

1 medium red onion, grated

4 cloves garlic, peeled and grated

½ cup fresh cilantro, finely chopped

1 tablespoon avocado oil

1 teaspoon salt

½ teaspoon ground pepper

Avocado oil for the grill

Whole grain buns

OPTIONAL TOPPINGS:

Lettuce

Tomatoes, sliced

Onions, sliced

Sliced Pickles

Ketchup and mustard

INSTRUCTIONS:

1. Mix turkey meat, grated onion, grated garlic, chopped cilantro, and avocado oil. Mix in salt and pepper.

2. Shape mixture into about 6 burgers (or more or less, depending on how large you want your burgers).

3. When ready to grill, prep the grill with avocado oil. Preheat grill to 400°F. Grill for about 6 minutes on each side. Use a meat thermometer to check that the internal temperature is over 165°F to ensure that the burgers are properly cooked.

4. Serve on whole-grain buns, with your desired toppings.

DINNER

Chicken Shawarma with Veggies

Makes: 4 servings

Difficulty:

This easy sheet-pan meal is the best! Just marinate the chicken in advance, assemble the ingredients, throw everything on a sheet pan, and bake, and you have a nourishing and delicious meal that's easy enough for a weeknight.

INGREDIENTS:

2 lemons, juiced

½ cup avocado oil

6 cloves garlic, peeled and grated

1 teaspoon salt

2 teaspoons black pepper

2 teaspoons ground cumin

2 teaspoons paprika

½ teaspoon turmeric

Red pepper flakes (optional to taste)

1 pound boneless skinless chicken breasts (preferably organic), cut into strips

1 large red onion, cut into quarters, with the layers separated to make chunky pieces

2 bell peppers, cut in large slices (red, orange, or yellow)

1 box (8 oz) mushrooms, sliced in half (optional)

INSTRUCTIONS:

1. Assemble marinade with lemon juice, avocado oil, grated garlic, salt, pepper, cumin, paprika, turmeric, and red pepper flakes (optional).

2. Add chicken strips. Cover and refrigerate for at least 4 hours, or overnight.

3. When ready to cook, heat the oven to 425°F and use a small amount of avocado oil to grease a baking sheet. Arrange marinated chicken strips on the baking sheet.

4. Add onion pieces, bell pepper pieces, and mushroom pieces to the leftover marinade. Toss until they are slightly coated.

5. Add vegetables to the baking sheet.

6. Bake for about 20-30 minutes, or until chicken is cooked and veggies are roasted. Use a meat thermometer to ensure the chicken reaches 165°F.

7. Serve chicken and veggies with whole-grain pita bread or brown rice and cucumber raita (recipe on page 102).

Adapted from a popular NY Times recipe by Sam Sifton

DINNER

Good Energy Lentil Soup

Makes: 6-8 servings

Difficulty:

This Mediterranean-style lentil soup is packed with plant-based protein and fiber, making it a healthy and hearty meal for the whole family. It's simple to make, budget-friendly, and full of nutrients—perfect for busy weeknight dinners, and lunchtime leftovers, when you want something both delicious and nourishing.

INGREDIENTS:

1 cup brown lentils

2 tablespoons avocado oil

1 large red onion, chopped

4 stalks celery, chopped

4 cloves garlic, chopped

4 carrots, chopped

1 potato, chopped into bite sized pieces (optional)

1 teaspoon cumin seeds

1 teaspoon salt

Black pepper to taste

6 cups vegetable broth

1 box (10oz) baby spinach or baby kale

2 tablespoons lemon juice

INSTRUCTIONS:

1. Rinse and drain brown lentils.

2. Heat the avocado oil in a large pot over medium-high heat. Add the onions, celery, garlic, and carrots. Sauté until the onions are soft and translucent.

3. Add brown lentils and potatoes. Add cumin seeds, salt, and pepper. Sauté for 1 minute.

4. Add vegetable broth. Bring the soup to a boil, cover, and then reduce the heat to low.

5. Simmer for 30-45 minutes, or until lentils are soft and creamy.

6. Add spinach or kale leaves. Stir in the greens until they have completely wilted. Add lemon juice.

7. Serve lentil soup with a hearty whole-grain bread.

WHY LENTILS?

Lentils are tiny but mighty! They are packed with plant-based protein, fiber, and minerals like iron, folate, and magnesium. Not only that, but they are quick to cook, budget-friendly, delicious, and will keep you nourished and full.

DINNER

PLANT BASED

Totally Awesome Tofu and Veggie Stir Fry

Makes: 6-8 servings

Difficulty: ★ ★ ★

This tofu and veggie stir fry is quick, colorful, and packed with flavor. It's a lighter, healthier take on takeout that comes together fast, making it a perfect weeknight meal for busy families.

INGREDIENTS:

FOR THE TOFU:

2 packages (each 14 oz) extra firm tofu (organic)

2 tablespoons avocado oil

½ teaspoon salt

½ teaspoon pepper

1 tablespoon soy sauce

2 cloves garlic, peeled and grated

1 inch piece ginger, peeled and grated

4 green onions, chopped

FOR THE VEGGIES:

4 tablespoons soy sauce

1 tablespoon honey or brown sugar

2 teaspoons toasted sesame oil

2 cloves garlic, peeled and grated

1 inch piece ginger, peeled and grated

½ teaspoon red pepper flakes

2 tablespoons avocado oil

2 bell peppers (yellow, red, or orange), chopped

3 cups broccoli, chopped

1 cup sugar snap peas

1 cup carrots, chopped

8 oz mushrooms, chopped

INSTRUCTIONS:

1. Prepare tofu by draining and then patting dry with paper towels. Wrap each block of tofu with a double layer of paper towels and press down gently to squeeze out the water. Cut tofu into ¾ inch cubes.

2. Heat avocado oil, salt, and pepper on medium-high in a wok or cast-iron pan. Add tofu pieces. Sauté for about 10 minutes, turning intermittently, until the tofu is lightly browned on all sides. Add 1 tablespoon soy sauce, garlic, ginger, and green onions. Sauté for 1-2 minutes and remove from the pan.

3. Assemble the stir-fry sauce by combining the soy sauce, honey, sesame oil, garlic, ginger, and red pepper flakes.

4. Heat 2 tablespoons of avocado oil on medium-high heat in a work or cast-iron pan. Add bell peppers, broccoli, snap peas, carrots, and mushrooms. Sauté and cook for about 5 minutes, until the veggies are slightly softened.

5. Reduce the heat to medium and add the stir-fry sauce. Stir and cook for 1-2 minutes, until the sauce thickens, and the vegetables are cooked but still tender. Add the cooked tofu to the veggies. Mix and add additional salt, pepper, and crushed red pepper to taste.

6. Serve with brown rice.

DINNER   **PLANT BASED**

Build-Your-Own Family Pizza

Makes: 2-4 servings

Difficulty:

Pizza night is more fun when everyone gets to play chef. With a ready-made whole wheat crust, all you need to do is pile on your favorite toppings and let the oven do the magic. Perfect for kids, weeknights, or anytime you want a healthier version of pizza without the fuss.

INGREDIENTS:

1 premade pizza crust (preferably 100% whole wheat)

About ½–¾ cup pizza sauce (preferably sugar free and made with just tomatoes, olive oil, and spices)

1 cup shredded mozzarella cheese

Toppings (choose your favorites):

Fresh vegetables: mushrooms, bell peppers, onions, spinach, zucchini, olives

Fresh herbs: basil, oregano

Proteins: grilled chicken, cooked beans, roasted chickpeas, turkey pepperoni, sausage, or other meats

INSTRUCTIONS:

1. Preheat the oven according to the crust package directions.

2. Spread the sauce evenly over the crust.

3. Sprinkle on the cheese, then add your favorite toppings!

4. Bake until the cheese is melted and the edges are crisp.

5. Slice it up, share, and enjoy.

TIP:

Choosing Your Toppings:

Fresh vegetables and lean proteins (like mushrooms, bell peppers, onions, olives, garlic, chicken, or even roasted chickpeas) bring big flavor, color, and nutrition to your pizza without weighing it down. Herbs like basil or oregano add amazing flavor, too.

Pepperoni and sausage can absolutely be enjoyed sometimes, too. They are classics for a reason! But if you're looking for everyday options, loading up on veggies or lighter proteins is a healthier way to go.

DINNER

The Greatest Grilled Salmon

Makes: 4-6 servings

Difficulty:

This salmon marinade recipe is so easy and delicious, and it's kid-approved! Adding wild-caught salmon to your weekly rotation is a great way to eat more omega-3 fats and protein!

INGREDIENTS:

¼ **cup soy sauce**

¼ **cup avocado oil**

1 **tablespoon brown sugar**

2 **inch section fresh ginger root, peeled and grated**

4 **cloves garlic, peeled and grated**

4 **pieces wild caught salmon**

Avocado oil for the grill

Lemons or limes for garnishing and serving (optional)

INSTRUCTIONS:

1. Assemble marinade with the soy sauce, avocado oil, brown sugar, grated ginger, and grated garlic. Arrange the salmon pieces in a single layer in a dish. Pour the marinade over the salmon, then gently turn the pieces to coat them evenly.

2. Marinate the salmon in the fridge for 30 minutes, up to 4 hours.

3. Prep grill with avocado oil to prevent sticking. Heat grill to 400°F. Grill salmon for 6 minutes on each side, starting with the skin side up. Transfer to a plate and cover with foil for 5 minutes before serving.

4. Squeeze lemon or lime juice on salmon, if desired, before serving.

WHY WILD CAUGHT SALMON?

Wild-caught salmon has more nutrients and less saturated fat than farm-raised, making it a healthier choice to eat. But getting sustainably caught wild salmon is also healthier for the Earth, because it avoids the pollution from fish farms and helps protect oceans, rivers, and the animals that live there.

DINNER

Nutrient Packed Chicken Noodle Soup

Makes: 8 servings

Difficulty: 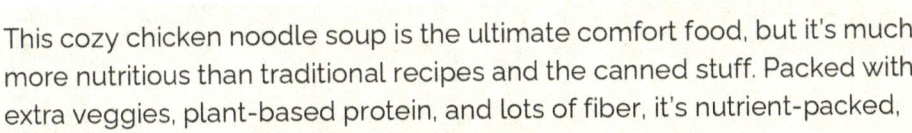 ⭐ ⭐ ⭐

This cozy chicken noodle soup is the ultimate comfort food, but it's much more nutritious than traditional recipes and the canned stuff. Packed with extra veggies, plant-based protein, and lots of fiber, it's nutrient-packed, delicious, and a complete meal.

INGREDIENTS:

2 tablespoons avocado oil

1 boneless, skinless chicken breast (about ½ pound), (preferably organic), chopped in small bite sized pieces

1 large red onion, chopped

4-5 stalks celery, chopped

4-5 large carrots, chopped

1 red bell pepper, chopped

1 box (8 oz) lentil or chickpea pasta

1 can (15.5 oz) chickpeas

10 cups vegetable broth

1 box (5 oz) baby kale (or spinach) leaves

1 teaspoon salt, to taste

½ teaspoon ground black pepper, to taste

INSTRUCTIONS:

1. Sauté the onion, celery, carrots, and chicken pieces in avocado oil until the onion is soft and translucent.

2. Add the bell pepper, salt, and pepper. Sauté for 1-2 minutes.

3. Add uncooked pasta and chickpeas, and then add the vegetable broth. Bring to a boil.

4. After the soup has boiled, turn down the heat to low and cover, and simmer for at least 20 minutes.

5. Add kale. Stir in the leaves until the kale has completely wilted. Serve immediately.

DINNER

Totally Epic Tacos

Makes: 6 servings

Difficulty:

These tacos are so delicious, and so healthy too! Loaded with flavor, every component (the meat, the beans, the corn, the guac, the pico, and the toppings) is delicious. Together, they are an incredible, balanced, family-friendly meal!

INGREDIENTS:

Taco Seasoning:
1 tablespoon chili powder
1 ½ teaspoons ground cumin
1 teaspoon smoked paprika
1 teaspoon garlic powder
1 teaspoon dried oregano
1 teaspoon salt
½ teaspoon black pepper
Pinch of red pepper or cayenne pepper (optional- depends on desired spice level and the spice level of your chili powder)

2 tablespoons avocado oil
½ onion, chopped
1 pound ground turkey breast (preferably organic)
1 can (14.5 oz) fire roasted diced tomatoes (or 2 fresh tomatoes, chopped)

1 bag (16oz) frozen corn
2 cans (15 oz each) black beans
½ teaspoon cumin
½ teaspoon salt

12 Soft Corn tortillas

Optional Toppings:
Cheddar cheese
Guacamole (see recipe page 124)
Pico de gallo (see recipe page 118)
Arugula, lettuce, or your favorite greens
Jalapeños

INSTRUCTIONS:

1. Mix all of the spices to make the taco seasoning. If desired, you can make a double or triple batch and store the leftover taco seasoning in a jar for next time. (If so, every time, use 3 tablespoons of the seasoning per 1 pound of the turkey meat.)

2. Heat a large skillet over medium-high heat. Add avocado oil, then the onion and turkey breast. Sauté until onions are slightly translucent and the turkey meat is cooked. Add 3 tablespoons of the taco seasoning. Mix. Add 1 can fire-roasted diced tomatoes or 2 fresh tomatoes. Cook the tomatoes in the meat mixture until the tomatoes soften and start to blend in.
Cover, and reduce the heat to low. Simmer for 10 minutes.

3. In a different saucepan, add rinsed and drained black beans. Add ¼ cup water, ½ teaspoon cumin, and ½ teaspoon salt. Stir. Heat until the beans are warm enough for serving.

4. In a microwave-safe dish, cook corn in the microwave per package instructions.

5. Lightly heat tortillas in a toaster oven, or on a dry skillet over medium heat for 30 seconds per side

6. To assemble tacos, take one corn tortilla, add cooked turkey meat, beans, corn, guacamole, pico, cheese, and greens. Enjoy!!

DINNER

Hidden Veggies Spaghetti and Meatballs

Makes: 6 servings (Plus freeze half of the meatballs for another dinner)

Difficulty:

Looking for a way to sneak in more veggies? These hidden veggie meatballs are delicious, moist, and kid-approved! Plus, with this recipe, you can make a big batch, use half of the meatballs right away, and then freeze the rest for an easy dinner another time.

INGREDIENTS:

FOR THE MEATBALLS:

4 large carrots (any color)

2 red, orange, or yellow bell peppers

1 large onion

2 teaspoons Italian seasoning

1 teaspoon black pepper

1 teaspoon salt

2 tablespoons flax seeds

1 lb ground turkey breast (preferably organic)

1 bottle pasta sauce (preferably made with just tomatoes, olive oil and spices)

1 box pasta (lentil or whole grain)

INSTRUCTIONS:

1. Preheat oven to 375°F. Prepare a baking sheet with aluminum foil, greased with a little bit of avocado oil.

2. Chop carrots, bell peppers, and onion into pieces that will fit into your food processor. Grind the veggies in the food processor until they are minced into very small pieces.

3. Combine minced vegetables with the Italian seasoning, pepper, salt, and flax seeds in a large mixing bowl. Add ground turkey breast. Mix well.

4. Shape into meatballs and place on a tray. Makes about 25-30, depending on your desired size. Bake at 375°F for 20-25 minutes, or until the internal temperature is 165°F.

5. Depending on the number of people you are serving, you may be able to use half or a third of the meatballs now and freeze the rest for later. (You can freeze the meatballs in a freezer-safe container or freezer-safe bags, for up to 2 months.)

6. Add the meatballs to the pasta sauce in a saucepan. Heat over medium heat until the sauce begins to boil.

7. Cook pasta according to directions on the package.

8. Serve the meatballs and sauce with the pasta.

DINNER

CHAPTER 4

SIDES

Wonderful Watermelon Salad

Makes: 8 servings

Difficulty:

This watermelon salad is so refreshing, so delicious, and so easy to make! Both a kid-favorite and crowd-favorite, this healthy side can be a summer staple.

INGREDIENTS:

¼ cup extra virgin olive oil

1 lemon juiced (about 4 tablespoons)

1 teaspoon salt

½ teaspoon freshly ground black pepper

1 small seedless watermelon, cut into cubes (about 7 cups)

1 cup Kalamata olives, chopped

1 small red onion, chopped

½ cup fresh basil, chopped

½ cup fresh mint, chopped

1 cup crumbled feta cheese (optional)

INSTRUCTIONS:

1. Whisk together the olive oil, lemon juice, salt, and pepper in a large bowl.

2. Add the watermelon, olives, onion, basil, and mint. Toss gently to combine.

3. Add the feta cheese, if desired, and mix gently.

4. Enjoy!

WHY WATERMELON?

Don't let its sweetness fool you—watermelon is a powerhouse fruit! It's loaded with water, fiber, and vitamins that keep you hydrated, support your immune system, and keep you energized. The bright red color comes from lycopene, an antioxidant that helps protect your body's cells and supports heart health. Every bite of this salad delivers vitamins and antioxidants that help your body thrive—plus, it's just plain delicious!

Adapted from a delightful watermelon salad made by Isaac Parlock

SIDES

PLANT BASED

Amazing Air Fryer French Fries

Makes: 4 servings

Difficulty:

These fries are crispy, golden, and full of flavor — no deep fryer needed! The best part? You don't even have to peel the potatoes. Leaving the skin on adds extra fiber, vitamins, and minerals, making your fries more nutritious (and a little extra crunchy, too). With just a few simple steps, you can turn plain potatoes into a snack that's both delicious and good for you.

INGREDIENTS:

2 medium russet potatoes, sliced into ¼ inch sticks. (no peeling necessary)

1 tablespoon avocado oil

½ teaspoon salt

Pinch of black pepper (optional)

INSTRUCTIONS:

1. Preheat your air fryer to 380°F (190°C). Wash and cut the potatoes into thin sticks — about ¼ inch thick — so they cook evenly.

2. Toss the fries in a bowl with avocado oil, salt, and black pepper.

3. Spread the fries in the air fryer basket in a single layer. Depending on the size of your air fryer, you might need to cook in batches.

4. Air fry for 12–15 minutes, shaking the basket halfway through, until the fries are golden and crispy.

5. Cool slightly, then dig in!

WHY POTATOES?

Potatoes are a great source of energy because they're complex carbohydrates, which help fuel your body and brain. They also contain vitamin C for strong immunity and potassium to help your muscles work their best. When cooked in the air fryer instead of deep-fried, they stay crispy without all the extra oil — a tasty and smart snack choice!

SIDES

PLANT BASED

Roasted Candied Carrots

Makes: 4 servings

Difficulty:

These carrots don't need any sugar to taste sweet — the oven does all the magic! When carrots roast, their natural sugars caramelize, turning them golden, tender, and full of flavor. They're like nature's candy: sweet, healthy, and totally snack-worthy. Whether you serve them with dinner or eat them right off the pan, these candied carrots will make you see veggies in a whole new way.

INGREDIENTS:

6-8 medium carrots (multicolored if possible), washed and cut (no peeling necessary)

1 tablespoon avocado oil

½ teaspoon salt

INSTRUCTIONS:

1. Preheat oven to 400°F. Line a baking sheet with parchment paper.

2. Toss sliced carrots in avocado oil, and then arrange on the baking sheet in a single layer. Sprinkle with salt.

3. Roast carrots for 20-25 minutes, or until carrots are slightly golden and cooked. Enjoy!

WHY CARROTS?

Carrots get their bright orange color from beta-carotene, a special nutrient your body turns into vitamin A. Vitamin A helps you see better in dim light and keeps your skin and immune system healthy. Carrots are also a good source of fiber, which helps your body digest food, and they taste naturally sweet when roasted. Every crunchy, colorful bite gives your body a boost!

SIDES

PLANT BASED

Sweet and Simple Strawberry Pecan Salad

Makes: 4-6 servings

Difficulty:

Here's a salad that proves healthy food can taste amazing! Sweet strawberries, crunchy pecans, nutrient-dense greens, and a light dressing come together for a mix of flavors and textures that's anything but boring. It's fresh, colorful, and easy to make-- but it's really pretty to look at too! Perfect for a weeknight dinner side, or even a weekend dinner party, this salad is kid-approved and healthy too!

INGREDIENTS:

5 oz fresh baby spinach

2 cups fresh strawberries, sliced

½ cup pecans, toasted or candied

2-3 radishes, thinly sliced

1 apple, core removed and cut in cubes

¼ cup dried cranberries (unsweetened)

Dressing (light vinaigrette)

3 tablespoons olive oil

1½ tablespoons apple cider vinegar

1 tablespoon Dijon mustard

1 ½ teaspoons honey

Salt and pepper to taste

INSTRUCTIONS:

1. Add baby spinach, strawberries, pecans, radish slices, apple pieces, and cranberries to a large salad bowl.

2. Whisk the olive oil, apple cider vinegar, mustard, honey, salt, and pepper together in a small measuring cup or bowl.

3. Drizzle the desired amount of dressing on individual salads.

4. Serve immediately.

WHY STRAWBERRIES?

Strawberries aren't just delicious — they're packed with nutrition, too. A single cup gives you more than your daily dose of vitamin C, supporting immunity and healthy skin. They're also rich in antioxidants that protect your cells, fiber that aids digestion, and nutrients that promote heart health. Best of all, they deliver all this goodness while staying naturally sweet and juicy.

SIDES

PLANT BASED

Cool and Delicious Cucumber Yogurt

Makes: 4 Servings

Difficulty:

Cool, creamy, and refreshing, cucumber yogurt (raita) is a classic Indian dish made with yogurt, cucumber, and a touch of spice. Traditionally served alongside curries and grilled meats, it balances bold flavors beautifully—but it's also delicious as a simple side or even a light snack on its own.

INGREDIENTS:

2 cups yogurt

½ large cucumber, grated

1 teaspoon salt

1 teaspoon cumin powder

INSTRUCTIONS:

1. Stir the yogurt until it is smooth and lump-free.

2. Mix in the grated cucumber, salt, and cumin powder.

3. Stir and garnish with a pinch of cumin powder.

4. Serve chilled.

TIP :

Cucumber raita makes the perfect partner for chicken shawarma (recipe on page 76). The cool, creamy yogurt balances the warm spices of the shawarma, for a delicious meal.

WHY YOGURT?

Yogurt isn't just creamy and delicious — it's also packed with good stuff for your body! It's full of protein to help build strong muscles and has calcium to keep your bones and teeth healthy.

Plus, yogurt has something called probiotics — tiny "good bacteria" that help keep your stomach happy and your digestion running smoothly. In recipes, yogurt adds a tangy flavor and creamy texture that can replace heavier ingredients like mayonnaise or cream. It's a simple way to make food taste great and feel good!

Simple Sautéed Spinach

Makes: 4 servings

Difficulty:

This quick recipe turns fresh spinach into something flavorful and full of nutrients. When you cook spinach with a little olive oil and garlic, it softens into a tasty side dish that goes with almost anything. It's one of the fastest veggies you can make — and it is so delicious!

INGREDIENTS:

1 tablespoon extra virgin olive oil

3 small cloves of garlic, minced

5 oz baby spinach leaves (about 6 cups)

¼ teaspoon salt

INSTRUCTIONS:

1. Heat olive oil in a skillet over medium heat. Add minced garlic, and cook for about 30 seconds.

2. Add the spinach leaves to the pan. It will look like a lot at first, but it will shrink quickly.

3. Reduce the heat to low and cover. Cook for 4-5 minutes, tossing occasionally, until all of the spinach leaves are wilted.

4. Remove from the heat once the spinach has wilted, but when it is still bright green. Sprinkle with salt and serve.

WHY SPINACH?

Spinach is packed with nutrients that help your body in amazing ways. It's full of iron, which helps your blood carry oxygen, and vitamin K, which helps your blood clot when you get a cut — and also helps keep your bones strong by working with calcium. Spinach is rich in vitamin A, too, which supports healthy eyes and skin. Even though it shrinks a lot when you cook it, every bite is loaded with nutrients your body needs to grow and stay healthy.

SIDES   PLANT BASED

Scrumptious Sweet Potato Fries

Makes: 4 Servings

Difficulty:

These sweet potato fries are golden, flavorful, and just a little bit sweet. With the air fryer doing all the hard work, you'll have a tasty snack that's fun to make and even more fun to eat.

INGREDIENTS:

2 sweet potatoes, sliced into ¼ inch sticks, (no peeling necessary)

1 tablespoon avocado oil

½ teaspoon salt

¼ teaspoon black pepper

¼ teaspoon garlic powder (optional)

¼ teaspoon paprika (optional)

INSTRUCTIONS:

1. Preheat air fryer oven to 375°F.

2. Toss sweet potato sticks with avocado oil, salt, and spices.

3. Arrange sweet potatoes in the air fryer basket, in a single layer, leaving space between the sweet potato sticks, so they are not touching.

4. Cook sweet potato fries in batches for approximately 12-15 minutes, shaking halfway. Cook until sweet potatoes are toasty brown and cooked.

5. Sprinkle with additional salt as needed. Serve immediately.

WHY SWEET POTATOES?

Sweet potatoes are a powerhouse food filled with nutrients your body needs to stay healthy. Their bright orange color comes from beta-carotene, a natural plant pigment that your body turns into vitamin A. Vitamin A is important for keeping your eyes sharp, your skin healthy, and your immune system strong.

Sweet potatoes also have fiber, which helps your stomach and intestines do their job, and complex carbohydrates, which give you steady energy that lasts. They're a great example of how delicious foods can also be super nutritious!

SIDES   PLANT BASED

The Easiest Lemony Cucumber Salad

Makes: 2-3 servings

Difficulty:

This crunchy cucumber side dish or snack is simple, delicious, and super refreshing! A squeeze of fresh lemon juice brightens up the flavor, while a sprinkle of salt and pepper makes it super tasty. It's a perfect, easy side, or quick snack for after school. With just a few ingredients, you can make a snack that's healthy, flavorful, and ready in minutes!

INGREDIENTS:

1 large cucumber, sliced

1 lemon

Salt and pepper to taste

INSTRUCTIONS:

1. Arrange cucumber slices on a plate.

2. Squeeze lemon juice on the cucumbers.

3. Sprinkle with salt and pepper to taste.

WHY CUCUMBERS?

Cucumbers are made of about 95% water, which makes them amazing for keeping your body hydrated. They're also a good source of vitamin K, which helps your blood clot properly and keeps your bones strong. Cucumbers have a light, refreshing taste because they're so full of water, and their crunch makes them a fun way to eat your veggies. Simple snacks like this one prove that healthy food can be cool, crisp, and totally delicious!

SIDES

PLANT BASED

Remarkable Roasted Broccoli

Makes: 4 servings

Difficulty:

When you roast broccoli, something amazing happens — the edges turn crispy, the inside gets tender, and the flavor becomes rich and slightly sweet. A little avocado oil, salt, and heat turn this everyday veggie into a snack or side dish you'll actually want seconds of. It's simple, colorful, and super good for you!

INGREDIENTS:

1 medium head of broccoli

1 ½ tablespoons avocado oil

½ teaspoon salt

¼ teaspoon black pepper

INSTRUCTIONS:

1. Preheat the oven to 400°F (220°C).

2. Toss the washed and dry broccoli with avocado oil, salt, and pepper in a large bowl until it's evenly coated.

3. Spread the florets out in a single layer on a baking sheet. Don't crowd them — space helps them crisp!

4. Roast for 18–22 minutes, stirring halfway through, until the tips are slightly brown and crispy.

TIP:

This recipe works great with other vegetables, too — try it with cauliflower or Brussels sprouts. They'll turn out just as crispy and delicious.

WHY BROCCOLI?

Broccoli is part of the cruciferous vegetable family, along with cauliflower, cabbage, and Brussels sprouts. These veggies are special because they contain phytonutrients — natural plant chemicals that help protect your body's cells from damage and keep you healthy.

One of the most powerful phytonutrients in broccoli is called sulforaphane, which helps all of your cells and supports a strong immune system. Broccoli is also rich in vitamin C, vitamin K, and fiber, which work together to keep your bones, blood, and digestion healthy. Eating cruciferous vegetables is one of the best things you can do for your health!

SIDES

PLANT BASED

Garlicky Green Beans

Makes: 4-6 servings

Difficulty:

These bright, crispy green beans are tossed in avocado oil and garlic for a quick, tasty side dish that's full of flavor. They're ready in minutes and keep their beautiful green color and crunch — no mushy beans here! Fast enough for weeknight dinners, but delicious enough for your holiday table, this recipe is healthy, tasty, and kid-approved.

INGREDIENTS:

16 oz fresh green beans

1 tablespoon avocado oil

4 cloves garlic, finely minced

2 tablespoons of water

½ teaspoon salt, and more to taste

INSTRUCTIONS:

1. Wash and prepare the green beans by cutting off the stems and tips.

2. Heat avocado oil in a skillet over medium heat. Add minced garlic, and cook for about 30 seconds.

3. Add green beans to the pan, and sauté for 2-3 minutes, until they look slightly seared — that means a few spots are a little darker, but the beans are still bright green.

4. Add 2 tablespoons of water, cover the pan, and turn the heat down to low. Cook for about 5 minutes, until the green beans are tender but still have a little crunch. They should stay a bright, beautiful green — that's how you know they're just right!

WHY GREEN BEANS?

You might think green beans are just another veggie, but there's a lot of science packed into those bright green pods! Their color comes from chlorophyll, the same pigment plants use to catch sunlight and make energy. That green color isn't just pretty — it's a sign of phytonutrients, special plant chemicals that help protect your cells and keep your body healthy. Green beans are also full of vitamin C to support your immune system, vitamin K to build strong bones, and fiber to keep your digestion on track. They're made up of more than 90% water, which helps keep you hydrated.

Fun Fact: Green beans aren't really beans at all — they're the unripe seed pods of the bean plant! If you left them on the vine, the pods would dry out and the beans inside would grow into full-sized seeds. Farmers pick them early so they stay crisp, tender, and full of nutrients.

SIDES

PLANT BASED

CHAPTER 5

SNACKS

Perfect Pumpkin Spice Muffins

Makes: 12 servings

Difficulty:

Looking for a perfect fall treat that's healthy too? These muffins are packed with protein and healthy fats, are refined sugar and refined flour-free, and they are kid-approved.

INGREDIENTS:

2 cups almond flour

2 heaping teaspoons pumpkin spice

1 heaping teaspoon cinnamon

½ teaspoon baking soda

½ teaspoon baking powder

½ teaspoon salt

3 eggs

1 cup canned pumpkin puree (not pumpkin pie filling)

½ cup pure maple syrup (not pancake or table syrup)

1 teaspoon pure vanilla extract

½ cup dark chocolate chips

½ cup chopped pecans for mixing (optional)

¼ cup chopped pecans for sprinkling (optional)

INSTRUCTIONS:

1. Mix the almond flour, pumpkin spice, cinnamon, baking soda, baking powder, and salt together in a medium bowl.

2. Mix the eggs, pumpkin, maple syrup, and vanilla together in a large bowl.

3. Mix the almond flour mixture into the pumpkin mixture. Stir in chocolate chips and pecans.

4. Line a muffin pan with paper liners (or grease it lightly). Scoop the batter into each cup, filling them about ¾ full. Sprinkle a few more pecans on the top of the muffins, if desired.

5. Bake at 350' F for 25 minutes, or until a toothpick inserted comes out clean. Cool for 10-15 minutes, and then enjoy!

6. Store in either ziplock bags or food storage containers for up to 1 week in the fridge.

Adapted from Almond Flour Pumpkin Muffins recipe by Layla Atik (Gimme Delicious)

SNACKS   GLUTEN FREE

Fresh and Simple Pico

Makes: 2-3 servings

Difficulty:

Why buy bottled salsa when homemade pico is so easy to make and even more flavorful? With just 5-6 ingredients, this pico can be thrown together in less than 10 minutes and is a perfect snack.

INGREDIENTS:

2 cups tomatoes, chopped (bright red Roma tomatoes, heirloom tomatoes, or multicolored grape tomatoes work well here)

½ cup green onions, chopped

¼ cup cilantro, chopped

3 tablespoons lime juice

Salt to taste

For spicy pico, you can add chopped fresh jalapeños to taste (optional)

INSTRUCTIONS:

1. Combine tomatoes, green onions, cilantro, and lime juice. Add salt and jalapeños to taste.

2. Serve with tortilla chips, for a snack. Or eat with tacos or quesadillas.

Irresistible Chocolate and Hazelnut Spread

Makes: 1 ½ cups

Difficulty:

This chocolate hazelnut spread is everything you love about the store-bought version, but made the way it should be—with simple, whole-food ingredients. It's creamy, chocolatey, and nutty, delicious on fruit, toast, or waffles, and fun for the whole family to enjoy together.

INGREDIENTS:

2 cups dry roasted and unsalted hazelnuts

1 teaspoon vanilla extract

¼ teaspoon kosher salt

⅓ cup powdered sugar

1 tablespoon avocado oil

3 tablespoons cocoa powder

1 cup dark chocolate chips

INSTRUCTIONS:

1. Process the hazelnuts in a food processor until they form a paste. Add the vanilla extract, salt, sugar, avocado oil, and cocoa powder. Blend until smooth.

2. Melt the chocolate chips in a microwave-safe bowl. Heat in 10–20 second intervals, stirring between each, until completely melted and smooth.

3. Add the melted chocolate to the food processor and blend again until the spread is smooth and creamy.

4. Transfer the chocolate hazelnut spread to a small glass jar. Store at room temperature and use within two weeks for the best flavor.

TIP:

Chocolate hazelnut spread is delicious with fresh fruit—try it with strawberries, apple slices, bananas, or pears. Honestly, just about any fruit pairs beautifully, so feel free to dip or drizzle your favorites. For extra fun, serve it alongside the rainbow fruit platter (recipe on page 148) —the two make a perfectly delicious pair.

Adapted from Simple Homemade Nutella recipe by Marzia (little spice jar)

SNACKS

PLANT BASED

The Greatest No-Bake Granola Bars

Makes: 15 servings

Difficulty:

These granola bars are so much healthier and more delicious than most store-bought kinds. Plus, they are fast to make, and the recipe can be customized with all of your favorite mix-ins.

INGREDIENTS:

2 cups old fashioned rolled oats

3 ½ cups mix-ins including: nuts, seeds, dried fruit, shredded coconut, or chocolate chips. (We like 2 cups sliced almonds, 1 cup shredded coconut, ½ cup dark chocolate chips)

2 teaspoons ground cinnamon

½ teaspoon salt

1 ½ cups creamy peanut butter, almond butter, or sunflower butter

½ cup pure maple syrup or honey

1 teaspoon vanilla extract

INSTRUCTIONS:

1. Combine the oats, mix-ins, cinnamon, and salt in a large mixing bowl.

2. Combine the peanut butter and maple syrup in a liquid measuring cup. Warm in the microwave in 15-second intervals, stirring between each, until the peanut butter is soft and the mixture is smooth. Stir in the vanilla extract.

3. Pour the peanut butter mixture over the oat mixture. Stir until fully combined.

4. Transfer the mixture to a 9×12-inch baking dish. Spread evenly and press down firmly to pack it in. Cover the dish.

5. Refrigerate overnight.

6. Cut into bars or squares, and individually wrap the bars in plastic wrap or baggies.

7. Store granola bars in the fridge and enjoy!

Adapted from Easy No-Bake Granola Bars recipe by Kathryne Taylor (Cookie and Kate)

SNACKS

PLANT BASED

Garden Fresh Guacamole

Makes: 4-6 servings

Difficulty: ★

Easy, fast, and delicious, homemade guacamole is a perfect snack! With just 5 ingredients, this guacamole is a breeze to whip up in 5 minutes.

INGREDIENTS:

3 medium sized avocados

½ cup red onion, chopped

¼ cup cilantro, chopped

5 tablespoons lemon juice

½ teaspoon salt (or more or less to taste)

INSTRUCTIONS:

1. Cut the avocados. (Cut each avocado lengthwise around the pit. Twist the halves to separate them. Use a spoon to remove the pit and the avocado.) Smash the avocados with a fork.

2. Add onion, cilantro, and lemon juice. Mix.

3. Add salt to taste.

4. Serve with tortilla chips, whole grain crackers, or vegetables. (Sliced cucumbers and carrots are great with this guacamole!)

SNACKS

PLANT BASED

Anytime Energy Trail Mix

Makes: 18 servings

Difficulty:

Most store-bought trail mixes have added oils on the dried fruit and nuts, which are not needed and not healthy! When you make your own, it's so fast and easy to make, plus it's so much healthier, less expensive, and more delicious than store-bought!

INGREDIENTS:

1 cup dry roasted, salted peanuts

1 cup unsalted raw almonds

1 cup raw walnuts

1 cup unsweetened dried cranberries

½ cup dark chocolate chips

½ teaspoon cinnamon

INSTRUCTIONS:

1. Mix nuts, dried cranberries, and chocolate chips in a mixing bowl. Add cinnamon.

2. Mix ingredients and store in a glass jar or individual plastic bags. Store trail mix in the fridge for optimal freshness.

TIP:

This recipe is so adaptable! Feel free to mix it up and substitute your favorite nuts for these ones. You can also add seeds (for example, pepitas and sunflower seeds) or different types of dried fruit.

If possible, try your best to use raw or dry-roasted nuts (not the kind with the added oils), and dried fruit that is unsweetened, unsulfured, and without added oil.

SNACKS

PLANT BASED

Homemade Hummus

Makes: 6 servings

Difficulty:

Do you know how easy it is to make hummus? You may even have all of the ingredients at home already. Hummus is such a tasty snack, and because it's mostly made of chickpeas and sesame seeds, it's healthy too.

INGREDIENTS:

¼ cup fresh lemon juice, from 1 large lemon

¼ cup tahini (well-stirred)

1 garlic clove

4 tablespoons extra-virgin olive oil, plus more for serving

½ teaspoon ground cumin

½ teaspoon salt or more to taste

¼ cup fresh cilantro (optional)

1 can (15 oz) chickpeas, rinsed and drained

2 to 3 tablespoons cold water

FOR SERVING:

Cucumber slices

Carrot chips

Bell pepper slices

Pita chips

INSTRUCTIONS:

1. Combine lemon juice and tahini in a food processor and process for 1 minute until they are well mixed and whipped.

2. Add garlic, olive oil, cumin, salt, and cilantro (optional). Process until well blended.

3. Add 1 can of rinsed chickpeas and process for 2 minutes, or until smooth. Add 2-3 tablespoons of cold water as needed to thin the hummus.

4. Serve with cucumbers, carrot chips, bell peppers, and pita chips.

TIP:

There are tons of flavor variations you can try that would be delicious too! Try adding an extra garlic clove for a stronger garlic flavor. Or if you like spice, add some red pepper flakes! Or try adding olives, roasted red peppers, or Zaatar spice.

Amazing Air-Fried Okra Fries

Makes: 4 servings

Difficulty:

This recipe was inspired by the crispy okra fries served at Chai Pani in Asheville, North Carolina, where they're dusted with chaat masala just before serving. Chaat masala is a tangy, slightly spicy Indian seasoning blend made with spices like cumin, coriander, dried mango powder (amchur), and black salt. It adds a punchy, savory-sour flavor that takes these fries in a bold, unexpected direction.

INGREDIENTS:

1 pound fresh okra, sliced horizontally to make "fries"

2 tablespoons avocado oil

Salt to taste

Chaat masala for sprinkling- optional

INSTRUCTIONS:

1. Preheat air fryer to 400°F.

2. Slice okra horizontally to make thin "fries." Drizzle okra fries with the avocado oil, and toss to evenly coat. Sprinkle with salt.

3. Cook okra fries in the air fryer for about 12 minutes, tossing once halfway through cooking.

4. Optional: Sprinkle "chaat masala" on the fries for extra flavor.

WHY OKRA FRIES?

Why not? If you've only met okra in a pot of gumbo or stew, these crispy fries will change the way you think about this veggie. Parents love that they're quick, easy, and healthier than a basket of drive-thru fries, while kids love that they're crunchy, dippable, and just plain delicious. These okra fries are proof that veggies can win over even the pickiest eaters.

Healthy Holiday Gingerbread Granola

Makes: 8 cups- about 16-24 servings

Difficulty:

Looking for a new, easy, and healthy holiday recipe? This holiday gingerbread granola, with red cranberries and green pumpkin seeds, is festive to look at and flavorful to eat! Packed with protein, healthy fats, and fiber, it's a snack that not only keeps you energized for the holidays but also makes you feel good from the inside out—comforted, satisfied, and ready to enjoy the season.

INGREDIENTS:

2 cups old-fashioned rolled oats

3 cups raw pecans

1 cup pepitas

1 cup unsweetened coconut flakes

1 teaspoon salt

1 teaspoon ground cinnamon

1 teaspoon ground ginger

1 tablespoon coconut oil

2 tablespoons real maple syrup

2 tablespoons molasses

1 teaspoon vanilla extract

½ cup dried cranberries (unsweetened)

⅓ cup candied ginger, chopped in small pieces

INSTRUCTIONS:

1. Preheat the oven to 350°F. Line a baking sheet with parchment paper.

2. Combine the oats, pecans, pepitas, coconut flakes, cinnamon, and ground ginger in a large mixing bowl.

3. Combine the coconut oil, maple syrup, and molasses in a small microwave-safe bowl.

4. Microwave in 10–15 second intervals, stirring between each, until the coconut oil has melted. Add the vanilla extract and stir.

5. Pour the coconut oil mixture over the granola mixture and stir until evenly coated. Spread in an even layer on the prepared baking sheet.

6. Bake for 10–15 minutes, or until the granola is lightly toasted. Add the dried cranberries and candied ginger, then stir to combine.

WHY GINGER?

Ginger adds a warm, spicy flavor that makes food taste cozy and comforting. But ginger is more than just delicious—it's been used for centuries to help soothe upset stomachs and support digestion. Ginger also contains antioxidants and natural compounds that can help your body fight off germs and feel its best. Even in small amounts, like the crystallized ginger pieces in this granola, it brings a little boost of flavor and feel-good benefits!

Adapted from Gingerbread Granola recipe by Kathryne Taylor (Cookie and Kate)

SNACKS

PLANT BASED

Always-Good Ants on a Log

Makes: 2 Servings

Difficulty:

Ants on a log is a healthy and easy snack that is fun to make! Plus, because it contains protein and healthy fats, it will keep you feeling energized and full all afternoon.

INGREDIENTS:

5 stalks celery

½ cup natural peanut butter or sunflower butter (unsweetened, and without added oils)

¼ cup raisins

INSTRUCTIONS:

1. Wash and cut celery stalks in half. (There is no need to peel the celery.)

2. Spread peanut butter on the celery and top with the raisins.

WHY PEANUT BUTTER?

Peanut butter is creamy, delicious, and packed with nutrients that give you lasting energy. It's full of plant-based protein, which helps build strong muscles, and healthy fats that keep you feeling full and fuel your brain. Peanut butter also provides vitamin E, magnesium, and potassium, which support your heart and overall health.

When you choose natural peanut butter made with just peanuts (and maybe a pinch of salt), you skip the added sugars and oils found in many brands, making it a tasty, wholesome choice for snacks, smoothies, or sandwiches!

WHY SUNFLOWER BUTTER?

Sunflower butter is a tasty, nut-free spread made from roasted sunflower seeds. It's packed with healthy fats, protein, and vitamin E, which helps protect your body's cells and keep your skin healthy. Sunflower butter also provides important minerals like magnesium and zinc for strong muscles and a healthy immune system. It's a great alternative for anyone with nut allergies and spreads just as creamy and delicious on toast, fruit, or in smoothies.

It is best to choose natural sunflower butter made with just sunflower seeds (and maybe a pinch of salt), and to skip the added sugars and oils found in many brands. This natural sunflower butter is not only healthier, but it's also delicious.

SNACKS   PLANT BASED

Irresistible Crunchy Kale Chips

Makes: 4 Servings

Difficulty:

These kale chips are an absolute favorite snack, and so easy to make. Crunchy, salty, and so flavorful– if you like them as much as we do, you may need to make a double batch!

INGREDIENTS:

1 bunch Tuscan or curly kale (or to make it even easier, use 1 bag of pre-washed, precut kale)

1 tablespoon extra virgin olive oil

½ teaspoon salt

¼ teaspoon red pepper (optional)

INSTRUCTIONS:

1. Preheat oven to 325°F.

2. If using a bunch of kale, wash and pat completely dry with paper towels. Remove the kale leaves from the thick stems, and tear into 2-inch pieces. Place in a large bowl.

3. If using precut, prewashed kale, place it in a large bowl.

4. Drizzle with olive oil and sprinkle with salt (and red pepper if using). Toss.

5. Arrange kale in a single layer on a baking sheet. Bake for 15-20 minutes, shaking halfway. Bake until chips are crunchy, but not burned.

WHY KALE?

Kale is part of the cruciferous vegetable family, along with broccoli, cauliflower, and Brussels sprouts. These veggies are packed with powerful nutrients that help your body stay strong and healthy. Kale is full of vitamins A, C, and K, which support your eyes, skin, and bones, and it's rich in fiber and calcium to keep your digestion and bones healthy.

Cruciferous vegetables also contain special plant compounds called glucosinolates, which help your body's natural defense systems protect your cells. Whether blended in a smoothie, baked into chips, or tossed into a salad, kale adds a tasty crunch and a big boost of green power to your plate!

Healthier Chocolate Milk

Makes: 4 Servings

Difficulty:

This chocolate milk is creamy, chocolatey, and naturally sweet—without all the extra sugar found in most store-bought versions. Instead of added sugars or syrups, it uses Medjool dates, which give a gentle, caramel-like sweetness along with fiber, potassium, and other nutrients. Unsweetened cacao powder adds rich chocolate flavor plus antioxidants that support your body's cells. And using soy milk makes it full of protein for growing bodies. It's a delicious way to treat yourself while giving your body something good!

INGREDIENTS:

2 cups soy milk (unsweetened and organic) or your preferred milk

3 pitted Medjool dates

2 tablespoons unsweetened cacao powder

INSTRUCTIONS:

1. Blend milk, dates, and cacao powder in a high-speed blender. For a sweeter flavor, add one more date and blend again.

2. Enjoy!

WHY SOY MILK?

Soy milk is a safe and healthy non-dairy option for kids because it has lots of protein to help them grow strong — almost as much as cow's milk! Eating soy has many health benefits, and soy milk is often fortified with calcium and vitamin D for strong bones and teeth.

Other non-dairy milks, like almond, oat, or rice milk, can be tasty too, but they usually have less protein and nutrients and often include more fillers or added ingredients.

For the healthiest choice, look for unsweetened, organic soy milk without extra flavors or additives.

SNACKS

PLANT BASED

CHAPTER 6

DESSERTS

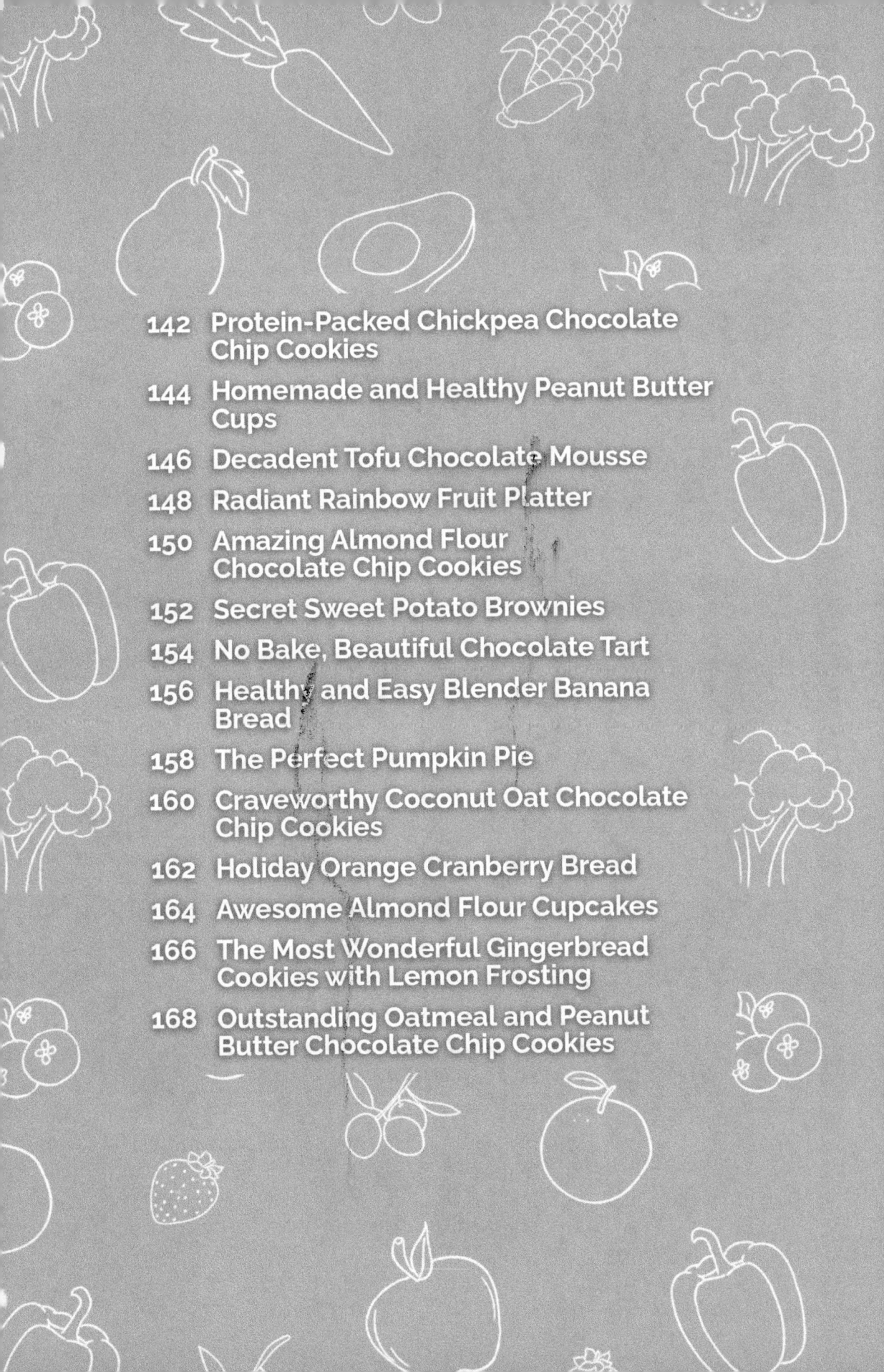

Protein-Packed Chickpea Chocolate Chip Cookies

Makes: 12 servings (1 cookie per serving)   **Difficulty:**

Why would anyone want to make cookies out of chickpeas? Good question!! Because they are absolutely delicious (you won't believe they are made of chickpeas), packed with protein, fiber-filled, gluten-free, nut-free, and bursting with nutrients. Don't believe me– just try them. You will not be disappointed!

INGREDIENTS:

½ **cup coconut oil, melted**

½ **cup coconut sugar**

2 eggs

1 teaspoon vanilla extract

1 ½ cups chickpea flour (also called garbanzo bean flour)

½ **teaspoon baking soda**

½ **teaspoon salt**

½ **cup dark chocolate chocolate chips**

INSTRUCTIONS:

1. Preheat oven to 350°F. Line a large baking sheet with parchment paper.

2. Mix coconut oil, sugar, eggs, and vanilla extract in a large bowl.

3. Mix the chickpea flour, baking soda, and salt together in a small bowl.

4. Add the dry ingredients to the wel ingredients and stir until a batter forms. Fold in the chocolate chips.

5. Using a tablespoon, drop cookie batter onto the baking sheet, making 12 cookies.

6. Bake at 350°F for 9-11 minutes, or until edges are golden brown.

7. Cool for 5 minutes before enjoying!!

Adapted from Chickpea Flour Chocolate Chip Cookies recipe by Monique Volz (Ambitious Kitchen).

DESSERT   **GLUTEN FREE**

Homemade and Healthy Peanut Butter Cups

Makes: 12 servings

Difficulty:

These peanut butter cups are so easy to make! Not only that, but they are refined sugar-free and made with whole food ingredients. They are a perfect treat!

INGREDIENTS:

Bowl 1:

1 cup peanut butter (use peanut butter made without added oils or sugar)

1 teaspoon vanilla extract

4 tablespoons real maple syrup (not table syrup)

2 tablespoons coconut oil (melted)

Bowl 2:

1 cup peanut butter (use peanut butter made without added oils or sugar)

1 teaspoon vanilla extract

4 tablespoons real maple syrup (not table syrup)

2 tablespoons coconut oil (melted)

6 tablespoons unsweetened cocoa powder

TIP:

Feel free to substitute almond butter for almond butter cups instead!

INSTRUCTIONS:

1. Line a muffin pan with 12 paper muffin liners.

2. Combine peanut butter, vanilla extract, maple syrup, and melted coconut oil in bowl one. (To melt the coconut oil, you can microwave the oil in a microwave-safe bowl for 10-15 seconds, or more if needed)

3. Combine peanut butter, vanilla extract, maple syrup, melted coconut oil, and cocoa powder in bowl two.

4. Drop 1 heaping tablespoon of mixture # 1 in each muffin tin. Flatten the mixture using the back of your spoon.

5. Drop 1 heaping tablespoon of mixture #2 in each muffin tin. Flatten the mixture using the back of your spoon.

6. Freeze for 1 hour.

7. Store the leftover peanut butter cups in a freezer-safe bag in the freezer. They make a perfect quick treat!

This recipe was adapted from Healthy Almond Butter Cups by Kathryn at Worn Slap Out

DESSERT   **PLANT BASED AND GLUTEN FREE**

Decadent Tofu Chocolate Mousse

Makes: 4 Servings

Difficulty:

This tofu chocolate mousse is every bit as decadent and delicious as the classic (which is typically made with heavy cream and eggs), but this healthier version is lighter, plant-powered, and packed with protein, so you can indulge without the heaviness.

INGREDIENTS:

1 ½ cups dark chocolate chips

1 package (16 oz) silken tofu (organic)

½ cup maple syrup

¼ cup soy milk (organic and unsweetened), or other preferred milk

1 teaspoon vanilla extract

⅛ teaspoon salt

INSTRUCTIONS:

1. Melt the chocolate chips in a microwave-safe bowl. Heat in 20-second intervals, stirring between each, until completely melted and smooth.

2. Add drained tofu, maple syrup, soy milk, vanilla, and salt to a high-powered blender. Blend until smooth.

3. Add melted chocolate chips and blend until smooth and silky.

4. Chill, and top with fruit for serving

WHY TOFU?

Tofu is made from soybeans, and soy is not only safe—it's a nutritious addition to any diet. It's a complete plant protein, giving your body all the essential amino acids it needs to build and repair muscles. Tofu is also naturally low in saturated fat and cholesterol-free, and it provides key nutrients like calcium and iron that support strong bones and steady energy.

And here's the truth about soy: despite the myths, research shows it's safe for both kids and adults—and a healthy way to add more plant power to your plate. For the best quality, look for organic tofu, which is made from non-GMO soybeans and grown without synthetic pesticides.

This recipe was adapted from Tofu Chocolate Mousse by Nora at Nora Cooks

DESSERT

PLANT BASED

Radiant Rainbow Fruit Platter

Makes: 8 Servings

Difficulty:

Bright, fresh, and bursting with color, a rainbow fruit platter is as beautiful as it is delicious. It's a simple way to bring variety to the table and makes healthy eating feel fun and inviting — perfect for kids and adults alike.

INGREDIENTS:

Red: 1 quart strawberries, cut in half or raspberries

Orange: 2 cups cantaloupe cubes or 4 mandarin oranges, peeled and segmented

Yellow: 2 cups mango cubes or pineapple chunks

Green: 1 cup green grapes or kiwi slices

Blue: 1 cup blueberries

Purple: 1 cup blackberries or red grapes

INSTRUCTIONS:

1. Arrange the fruit on a platter to make a rainbow.

2. Serve as a beautiful dessert, as a snack, or on the side of your breakfast, lunch, or dinner.

TIP:

A rainbow fruit platter isn't just pretty to look at — it's fun to make! A super fun project for families or kids, it doubles as a healthy treat. Prep one ahead of time and keep it in the fridge, and you'll find it gets eaten up for breakfast, snacks, lunch, and even dessert. Fresh, colorful, and inviting, it's the kind of dish that makes healthy eating feel effortless.

Amazing Almond Flour Chocolate Chip Cookies

Makes: 12 Servings

Difficulty:

Made with wholesome ingredients, these almond flour cookies are more nourishing than your average cookie, with less sugar and less oil. Plus, they are naturally gluten-free. But not to worry– these cookies taste amazing! They are kid-approved and every bit as delicious.

INGREDIENTS:

2 tablespoons coconut oil (melted)

¼ cup almond butter

1 egg

1 teaspoon vanilla extract

½ cup coconut sugar

½ teaspoon baking soda

¼ teaspoon salt

2 cups almond flour

½ cup dark chocolate chips

INSTRUCTIONS:

1. Preheat oven to 350˚F. Prepare a cookie sheet with parchment paper.

2. Mix wet ingredients: coconut oil, almond butter, egg, vanilla, and sugar. Stir well until completely mixed.

3. Add baking soda and salt. Stir to mix well.

4. Add almond flour. Mix well.

5. Stir in chocolate chips.

6. Use a tablespoon to drop cookie dough onto the prepared cookie sheet, making about 12 cookies.

7. Bake cookies for 10-12 minutes, or until the edges are starting to look light golden brown.

8. Cool for a few minutes before enjoying!

WHY ALMOND FLOUR?

Almond flour brings a naturally delicious flavor and chewy texture to cookies. It also adds protein, fiber, a natural sweetness, and healthy fats, making each bite more nutritious and satisfying, and reducing the need for added sugar and added oils.

This recipe was adapted from Almond Flour Cookies by Erin at Well Plated

DESSERT   GLUTEN FREE

Secret Sweet Potato Brownies

Makes: 12 Servings

Difficulty:

These sweet potato brownies are rich, fudgy, and naturally sweetened by a secret ingredient — mashed sweet potatoes! But don't worry- even the pickiest eaters will enjoy these. If you didn't know the secret ingredient, you'd never guess it was there.

INGREDIENTS:

1 cup sweet potato, cooked and mashed

½ cup peanut butter (or other nut butter of your choice)

¼ cup maple syrup

1 teaspoon vanilla extract

¼ cup almond flour (or oat flour if allergic)

¼ cup cocoa powder

½ cup dark chocolate chips

WHY SWEET POTATOES?

Sweet potatoes add natural sweetness, moisture, and a fudgy texture that makes these brownies irresistibly rich.

They're also nutrient powerhouses! Sweet potatoes are packed with fiber, vitamin A, vitamin C, potassium, and antioxidants, giving this delicious dessert a wholesome boost.

INSTRUCTIONS:

1. Preheat your oven to 350°F and prepare a brownie pan (9x9 inch works well) with parchment paper.

2. Use a fork to poke holes in a sweet potato (to let steam escape while cooking). Cook the sweet potato in the microwave for 5-8 minutes, turning halfway through, until it's very soft when pierced with a fork. (Time will vary depending on potato size and your microwave.)

3. Let the sweet potato cool slightly before slicing open and scooping out the flesh. Mash with a fork or potato masher until smooth.

4. While the sweet potato is cooking, mix the peanut butter, maple syrup, and vanilla extract in a bowl. Add the mashed sweet potato.

5. Mix in the almond flour and then the cocoa powder.

6. Stir in the chocolate chips. Transfer the mixture to the brownie pan

7. Bake at 350°F for about 30 minutes. Let the brownies cool before slicing and enjoying!

This recipe was adapted from Fudgy Sweet Potato Brownies by Carleigh at Plant You

DESSERT

PLANT BASED

No Bake, Beautiful Chocolate Tart

Makes: 12 Servings

Difficulty:

This chocolate tart is simple enough to make on a weeknight, but also beautiful enough to serve for a holiday dessert. Made with all whole food ingredients, no refined sugar, and loaded with antioxidants, this dessert is a perfect family-friendly treat.

INGREDIENTS:

For the crust:

1 ¾ cups almond flour

¼ cup unsweetened cocoa powder

¼ teaspoon salt

2 tablespoons pure maple syrup

¼ cup coconut oil (melted)

For the Filling:

6 oz bittersweet chocolate, finely chopped

¾ cup canned full-fat coconut milk

¼ teaspoon vanilla extract

2 tablespoons raspberry preserves (preferably without refined sugar)

2 tablespoons pomegranate juice

⅓ cup fresh pomegranate seeds and/or 1 cup fresh raspberries

INSTRUCTIONS:

1. Combine almond flour, cocoa powder, salt, maple syrup, and coconut oil to make the crust. Press the mixture evenly into a tart pan. Set aside.

2. Place finely chopped chocolate in a medium-sized bowl. In a separate bowl, microwave coconut milk until it starts to bubble and boil in the microwave. Pour the hot coconut milk over the chopped chocolate, and cover with a plate or plastic wrap. Let this sit for about 5 minutes, then whisk the chocolate and coconut milk mixture until creamy. Whisk in vanilla extract, raspberry preserves, and pomegranate juice. Pour the filling into the prepared crust. Cover with foil or plastic wrap.

3. Place the tart in the refrigerator and let it cool for at least 1-2 hours. Sprinkle pomegranate seeds and/or raspberries on top before serving.

WHY DARK CHOCOLATE?

Chocolate, especially dark chocolate, is rich in antioxidants called flavonoids. These powerful compounds help protect the body's cells from damage, and they're linked to benefits like supporting heart health and circulation. The higher the cocoa content, the more antioxidants chocolate contains, making bittersweet chocolate or dark chocolate a better choice when you want both flavor and a little nutritional boost.

This recipe was created by the very talented Kathryn at Worn Slap Out

DESSERT   PLANT BASED

Healthy and Easy Blender Banana Bread

Makes: 12 servings

Difficulty:

This banana bread couldn't be easier to make, and it's essentially refined sugar, refined flour, and oil-free! But the best part is, it's kid-approved and absolutely delicious!

INGREDIENTS:

2 cups rolled oats (preferably organic)

4 large bananas

2 eggs

6 tablespoons honey

1 teaspoon cinnamon

¼ cup soy milk (organic and unsweetened). If preferred, you can also use a different non-dairy milk of your choice

1 teaspoon baking soda

½ cup chocolate chips (preferably dark chocolate)

½ cup walnuts (optional)

INSTRUCTIONS:

1. Preheat oven to 350°F. Very lightly grease a loaf pan.

2. In a high-speed blender or food processor, add the oats, bananas, eggs, honey, cinnamon, soy milk, and baking soda.

3. Blend until the mixture is smooth. If the batter is too thick and is not mixing properly, you can add a little bit more soy milk.

4. Stir in chocolate chips and walnuts.

5. Pour mixture into the prepared loaf pan. Bake for 35-40 minutes, or until a toothpick comes out clean.

6. Store covered in the refrigerator for up to 1 week (if it lasts that long).

TIP:
Feel free to substitute other nuts instead of the walnuts

DESSERT

GLUTEN FREE

The Perfect Pumpkin Pie

Makes: 8 servings

Difficulty:  ★ ★ ★

Sweetened with dates and maple syrup, this pumpkin pie is so much healthier than the store-bought kinds, but it tastes just as delicious. Plus, the healthy pie crust is so easy to make– it really is a perfect recipe!

INGREDIENTS:

4 dates
⅓ cup soy milk (unsweetened and organic), or other preferred milk
¼ cup pure maple syrup (not table or pancake syrup)
1 can (15 oz) pumpkin puree
3 eggs
1 teaspoon vanilla extract
1 heaping teaspoon cinnamon
2 heaping teaspoons pumpkin pie spice
¼ teaspoon salt

Crust
1 ½ cups almond flour
¾ cup whole wheat pastry flour
½ teaspoon salt
2 tablespoons coconut sugar
8-10 tablespoons of unsweetened, organic soy milk (or other non-dairy milk of choice)

INSTRUCTIONS:

1. Lightly grease a pie pan with avocado oil. Preheat oven to 350°F.

2. Soak 4 dates in hot water for about 10 minutes, while you are making the pie crust.

3. To make the pie crust, mix almond flour, pastry flour, salt, and coconut sugar in a mixing bowl. Add the soy milk gradually, mixing intermittently. When you get to the 7th tablespoon, add the remaining milk 1 tablespoon at a time, mixing after each time. Add enough milk so the crust is moist and can be rolled out, without it being too wet or sticky.

4. Roll out the crust on a piece of parchment paper, using extra pastry flour as needed to prevent the dough from sticking to the rolling pin. Transfer the crust to the slightly greased pie pan. Trim the edges with a knife, and crimp the edges with your fingers. (Alternatively, the pie crust can also be shaped in the pie pan with your hands, instead of rolling it out.)

5. In a blender, combine the soy milk, drained dates (discard the soaking water), and maple syrup. Blend until the dates are completely broken down and the mixture is smooth.

6. Mix the pumpkin puree, eggs, maple syrup/date mixture, vanilla extract, cinnamon, pumpkin pie spice, and salt in a large mixing bowl,

7. Whisk the pumpkin filling until it is smooth and creamy. Pour the pumpkin pie filling into the pie crust.

8. Bake for 50-60 minutes until the filling is no longer liquid. Keep an eye on the pie crust while baking and cover the edges with foil, if needed, to prevent the crust from burning.

9. Cool pie for at least an hour before cutting and serving. Store leftovers in the refrigerator.

DESSERT

Craveworthy Coconut Oat Chocolate Chip Cookies

Makes: 12 cookies

Difficulty:

These craveworthy cookies are healthier than most because they are made with nourishing rolled oats, plus they have less saturated fat and less sugar than typical store-bought cookies, and they are gluten-free. But not only that, these cookies are super delicious, and kid-approved!

INGREDIENTS:

¼ **cup coconut oil**

1 egg

½ **cup coconut sugar**

1 teaspoon vanilla extract

1 cup rolled oats for oat flour

½ **cup rolled oats**

½ **cup unsweetened shredded coconut**

½ **teaspoon baking soda**

¼ **teaspoon salt**

½ **cup dark chocolate chips**

INSTRUCTIONS:

1. Preheat oven to 350°F. Line a baking sheet with parchment paper.

2. Melt coconut oil by putting it in the microwave for 15-20 seconds.

3. Mix together 1 egg, melted coconut oil, coconut sugar, and vanilla extract in a large mixing bowl,

4. Make oat flour by grinding 1 cup of rolled oats in a blender or food processor until the oats have turned to flour.

5. Mix oat flour, rolled oats, shredded coconut, baking soda, and salt.

6. Mix the oat flour mixture with the wet ingredients. Mix well. Stir in chocolate chips.

7. Transfer to the baking sheet using a tablespoon of batter for each cookie. Space cookies at least 2 inches apart.

8. Bake for 9-12 minutes, or until edges are golden brown.

Recipe adapted from Healthy Oatmeal Chocolate Chip Cookies by Monique Volz from Ambitious Kitchen

DESSERT   **GLUTEN FREE**

Holiday Orange Cranberry Bread

Makes: 12 servings

Difficulty:

This cranberry orange bread is a festive treat for the holidays, which is bursting with delicious flavors. Made with whole wheat flour and less sugar than most store-bought desserts, this treat is healthier than most, but kid-approved.

INGREDIENTS:

1 ½ cups whole wheat flour
1 teaspoon baking powder
1 teaspoon baking soda
½ teaspoon salt
1 tablespoon orange zest
2 oranges, preferably organic, juiced- about ¾ cup orange juice
½ cup sugar
¾ cup unsweetened applesauce
2 eggs
1 ½ cups chopped frozen cranberries
½ cup chopped walnuts or pecans (optional)

INSTRUCTIONS:

1. Grease a 9-inch x 5-inch loaf pan with avocado oil. Preheat oven to 350°F.

2. Mix whole wheat flour, baking powder, baking soda, and salt in a mixing bowl.

3. Using a zester, zest 2 oranges to get 1 tablespoon orange zest. Squeeze the oranges to get about ¾ cup of orange juice.

4. Mix the sugar, applesauce, orange juice, orange zest, and eggs together in a large mixing bowl until well combined.

5. Add flour mixture to wet ingredients and stir until well mixed. Stir in frozen cranberries and nuts.

6. Transfer the batter to the prepared loaf pan.

7. Bake for 55-60 minutes, or until a toothpick inserted into the center of the bread comes out clean.

WHAT IS ORANGE ZEST?

Zest is the thin, colorful outer layer of citrus fruits like lemons, limes, and oranges. It's packed with tiny oils that give off bright, fresh flavor, even stronger than the juice!

To get the zest, gently scrape or grate just the colored part of the peel using a zester or fine grater. Be careful not to go too deep — the white part underneath (called the pith) tastes bitter. Tip: It's best to use organic citrus when you're zesting. That's because the peel, where the zest comes from, can hold onto waxes or pesticides that are sometimes used on non-organic fruit. If you can't find organic, wash and scrub the fruit really well before zesting.

Recipe adapted from My Healthy Cranberry Orange Bread from Avery's Kitchen Dance

DESSERT

Awesome Almond Flour Cupcakes

Makes: 12 servings

Difficulty:

These chocolate cupcakes are healthier than most because they are refined flour-free, they have less sugar than the store-bought kinds, and they contain protein and healthy fats from the almond flour. Plus, the homemade hazelnut and chocolate spread makes a delicious and decadent frosting!

INGREDIENTS:

1 ⅓ cups almond flour

½ cup arrowroot starch

½ cup cacao powder

½ teaspoon baking soda

¼ teaspoon salt

¾ cup coconut sugar

¼ cup honey

½ cup full fat canned coconut milk

2 eggs

¼ cup avocado oil

1 teaspoon vanilla extract

1 teaspoon apple cider vinegar

INSTRUCTIONS:

1. Preheat oven to 350°F. Line a muffin tray with 12 muffin liners.

2. Mix almond flour, arrowroot starch, cacao powder, baking soda, and salt in a mixing bowl.

3. Combine coconut sugar, honey, coconut milk, eggs, avocado oil, vanilla extract, and apple cider vinegar in a large mixing bowl.

4. Add dry ingredients to the wet ingredients. Mix until it forms a smooth batter.

5. Add batter to the muffin cups. Fill each muffin cup ⅔ of the way up. Bake for 20-24 minutes, or until a toothpick comes out clean. Cool.

6. After cupcakes are cool, frost with homemade hazelnut and chocolate spread (recipe on page 120).

Recipe adapted from Almond Flour Chocolate Cupcakes by Claire Cary from Eat with Clarity.

DESSERT   **GLUTEN FREE**

The Most Wonderful Gingerbread Cookies with Lemon Frosting

Makes: 20 servings

Difficulty:

These amazing gingerbread cookies taste like the holidays. They are warm, cozy, and full of spice, but they also have a delicious hint of lemony brightness on top. Made with almond flour, they're naturally healthy and delicious, with just the right sweetness for celebrating or snacking any time of year.

INGREDIENTS:

3 cups almond flour

½ cup arrowroot starch

4 teaspoons ground ginger

1 teaspoon ground cinnamon

¼ teaspoon ground cloves

¼ teaspoon fine sea salt

½ teaspoon baking powder

4 tablespoons melted coconut oil

½ cup pure maple syrup

2 tablespoon blackstrap molasses

Lemon Icing:

2 tablespoons lemon juice

6 tablespoons powdered sugar

INSTRUCTIONS:

1. Preheat oven to 350°F. Line a baking sheet with parchment paper.

2. Combine almond flour, arrowroot starch, ginger, cinnamon, cloves, salt, and baking powder in a large mixing bowl.

3. Add in coconut oil, maple syrup, and molasses, and mix until the dough is formed.

4. Refrigerate for 1 hour, up to overnight, to chill the dough.

5. Roll out the dough, approximately ¼ inch thick, on parchment paper, using flour as needed to prevent sticking. Use cookie cutters to make your desired shapes and transfer them to the tray. The dough should make about 20-25 cookies.

6. Bake cookies for 10 minutes, or until edges are golden brown.

7. Cool cookies. To frost them, mix lemon juice and powdered sugar in a small bowl. Apply a thin layer of icing to each cookie. Enjoy!

Recipe adapted from Megan Gilmore's Almond Flour Gingerbread Cookies from Detoxinista

DESSERT **GLUTEN FREE**

Outstanding Oatmeal and Peanut Butter Chocolate Chip Cookies

Makes: Makes 18 cookies

Difficulty:

These cookies are chewy, chocolatey, and full of peanut buttery goodness, all without a single scoop of flour! Oats give them a soft, hearty texture, while peanut butter holds everything together and adds a rich, nutty flavor. They're naturally sweet, easy to make, and perfect for an after-school snack or a healthy dessert. With melty chocolate chips in every bite, these cookies prove that simple, whole food ingredients can make something seriously delicious.

INGREDIENTS:

¾ cups rolled oats (preferably organic)

½ teaspoon baking soda

1 cup peanut butter (made with just peanuts and salt)

½ cup coconut sugar

1 teaspoon vanilla extract

2 eggs

⅔ cup dark chocolate chips

INSTRUCTIONS:

1. Preheat the oven to 350°F. Line a baking sheet with parchment paper.

2. Mix the oats and baking soda together in a small bowl.

3. Combine the peanut butter, coconut sugar, vanilla, and eggs in a large bowl. Add the oat mixture and stir until a dough forms.

4. Fold in the chocolate chips.

5. Scoop the dough onto the prepared baking sheet using a tablespoon. Bake for 9–12 minutes, or until the bottom edges are lightly golden.

6. Cool the cookies on the baking sheet for at least 10 minutes before enjoying.

Recipe adapted from Monique Volz's Flourless Peanut Butter Oatmeal Chocolate Chip Cookies recipe on Ambitious Kitchen

DESSERT   **GLUTEN FREE**

ABOUT THE AUTHORS

Dr. Ritu Saluja-Sharma, MD, is a double board-certified physician in Emergency Medicine and Lifestyle Medicine, a mom, and the founder of Head Heart Hands—a comprehensive, holistic wellness program for individuals and organizations.

After years of practicing Emergency Medicine on the frontlines of our healthcare system and seeing many of her patients suffering with diseases that could likely have been prevented (and many which could potentially still be reversed), Dr Saluja-Sharma earned a second board certification in Lifestyle Medicine and created Head Heart Hands to help adults prevent and reverse disease by targeting ROOT CAUSES.

Her programs are designed to help participants lower their blood sugars, blood pressure, and cholesterol, increase their energy, improve their mood, decrease their pain, and improve their quality of life. As more and more adults have experienced incredible health transformations through her programs, they have frequently shared how they wished they had this help when they were younger. Teachers and principals have shared that they wish their students could learn the same tools and insights. Their experiences have inspired her to expand her focus to children, to help the next generation build strong, healthy foundations—starting when it matters most.

Through her book, companion workbook, and cookbook, she's empowering a new generation to understand the power of food, build healthy mindsets, and fall in love with their bodies and the nourishment that fuels them. She is currently working to improve the health and nutrition curriculum in public schools and serves as an expert advisor on state-level curriculum standards.

Serena Sharma

Serena is the co-author of The Wonder of What We Eat Cookbook. Serena helped to create the kid-approved recipes and take photos of our creations. Serena's interest in cooking and taking photos inspired her to work on this project. Serena also enjoys soccer and art.

KEEP LEARNING, KEEP GROWING!

Loved this cookbook? There are 2 companion books to explore!

The Wonder of What We Eat: How Our Incredible Food, Our Incredible Bodies, and Our Incredible Planet Are Connected

The Wonder of What We Eat is a science-based, beautifully illustrated book that helps kids discover how food powers their body, brain, mood, and even the planet—all while building a healthy relationship with food, a positive body image, and a sense of empowerment over their own health.

Written by a physician and mom, this unique guide goes beyond the basics of "eat your veggies" and introduces kids to powerful concepts that even most adults haven't learned, including:

- **Eye-opening nutrition science** — like how food affects your microbiome, genetics, metabolism, energy, emotions, and even the planet
- **A fresh, empowering mindset around food and the body** — replacing diet culture with a focus on nourishment, self-care, and resilience
- **Essential health literacy skills** — including decision-making, goal-setting, and analyzing influences
- **Encouragement and real-life tools** — giving kids confidence and practical strategies they can use every day to expand their food choices, support healthy growth, and build habits that can help with picky eating and maintaining a healthy weight
- **A positive, shame-free approach** — helping kids build a healthy relationship with food, understand their bodies, and make choices that help them thrive, now and for the future

By giving kids practical nutrition knowledge, a healthy mindset about food and their bodies, and the tools to make positive changes, we can literally change the trajectory of their health—and their lives.

Ready to raise a generation that's informed, empowered, and excited about their health? Start here—with *The Wonder of What We Eat*.

KEEP LEARNING, KEEP GROWING!

Loved this cookbook? There's more to explore!

The Wonder of What We Eat Cookbook is just the beginning. Keep the journey going with these two exciting companions:

The Wonder of What We Eat Workbook: Activities and Reflections to Help Kids Build Healthy Habits and a Positive Relationship with Food
By Ritu Saluja-Sharma, MD and Dylan Sharma

The Wonder of What We Eat Workbook is the hands-on companion to the science-based, beautifully illustrated book.

Created by a physician and mom, this workbook helps kids:

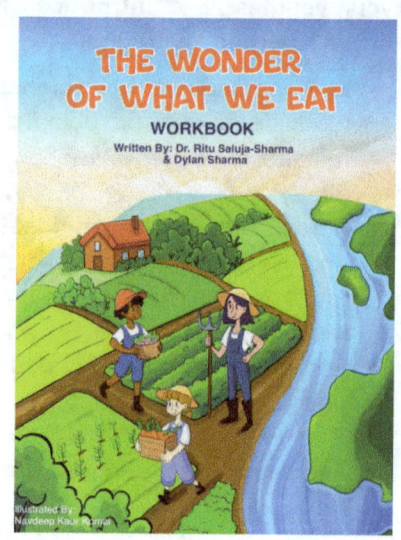

- **Put nutrition knowledge into action**—with fun activities, real-life label reading, powerful reflections, and creative goal-setting, to help kids apply what they have learned and develop positive eating habits.

- **Build a healthy mindset around food and the body**—developing a positive relationship with food while replacing diet culture with nourishment, empowerment, self-care care and a positive body image

- **Practice real-world health literacy skills**—like decision-making, analyzing influences, and making thoughtful choices

- **Feel confident and capable**—with encouraging prompts, simple strategies, and hands-on learning of essential nutrition concepts.

- **Support common challenges**—offering a supportive, shame-free alternative to help with picky eating, weight concerns, and early health challenges

Whether used at home, in classrooms, or with health professionals, this workbook is already making an impact. Lessons are currently being used in one of the largest public school systems in the country—bringing engaging, prevention-focused health education to thousands of students.

Ready to turn knowledge into real-life transformation?

Take the next step—with *The Wonder of What We Eat Workbook.*

FOR GROWN-UPS WHO WANT TO FEEL BETTER, TOO

If this book inspired you to think differently about food and health for your kids, you're not alone. Many adults reading this have asked the same question: "Where was this information when I was growing up?"

The truth is—it's never too late to start.
Dr. Ritu Saluja-Sharma, the author of The Wonder of What We Eat, is also the founder of **Head Heart Hands**.

What is Head Heart Hands?

It's an evidence-based, physician-created, proven, step-by-step program addressing all aspects of health including insulin resistance, inflammation, nutrition, and weight loss, but also stress, sleep, and mental health, designed to help you lose weight, increase your energy, and lower your blood sugars, cholesterol, and blood pressure in 12 Weeks.

Head: Step-By-Step Guidance and Mindset: Understand the Root Causes of our most common physical and mental health disorders. Learn how to target those root causes to help you lose weight, increase your energy, lower your blood sugars, decrease your cholesterol, and reduce your blood pressure, without medications.

Heart: Hope and Support: Our bodies are powerful and miraculous and are often capable of healing themselves. Improve your relationship with food, your body, and your health. Ditch dieting and instead focus on nourishment and self-care.

Hands: Tools and Reach: Implement positive changes into your life by using the many tools from this program, including meal plans, recipes, grocery lists, and challenges. Transcend the confines of hospitals and doctors' offices to meet you where you are- at school, at work, and at home.

Learn More

To explore online adult programs, corporate wellness, and hospital or school system partnerships visit headhearthandsmd.com. Or follow along on Instagram: @head_heart_handsmd

A 12 WEEK JOURNEY OF WELLNESS AND WEIGHT LOSS

www.ingramcontent.com/pod-product-compliance
Lightning Source LLC
Chambersburg PA
CBHW080901120626
46555CB00008B/2908